日本の扇子の歴史

—西洋にもたらしたその影響—

ŌGI

A HISTORY OF THE
JAPANESE FAN

© 1992
Dauphin Publishing Limited

World copyright reserved.

Hutt, Julia
Alexander, Hélène
ŌGI: A History of the Japanese Fan

British Library Cataloguing in Publication Data
A catalogue record for this book
is available from the British Library.

ISBN 1-872357-08 3

Published by Dauphin Publishing Limited.

First Published in April 1992.

Designed and printed by Dauphin Publishing Limited.
118A Holland Park Avenue, London, W11 4PA.

Printed and bound in Great Britain.

ŌGI

A HISTORY OF THE
JAPANESE FAN

Julia Hutt & Hélène Alexander

Dedication

The authors wish to dedicate this book, with much special affection and appreciation to

MRS BETTY HODKINSON MBE.

A trustee of The Fan Museum, she has devoted long hours, beyond the call of duty, never flinching at any of the unpleasant, tiring and often tedious tasks associated with identifying many of the fans, having texts translated and keeping a vigilant eye on the day-to-day running of The Fan Museum.

Acknowledgements

The authors wish to express their grateful thanks to the following people for their invaluable help with the painstaking research and production of this work:

The Exhibition Committee of Honour comprising Sir Arthur Drew, Sir John Figgess KBE, CMG, Christopher Western and David Brewer, each one of them giving invaluable advice and encouragement;

Dicky Alexander CBE, Chairman of The Fan Museum Trust, for his skill and diplomacy in bringing together so many of the exterior elements of this book;

Caroline Allington, whose conservation skills were more than once put to task with 'a stitch in time';

Sir Hugh Cortazzi for his wise advice and kind remarks;

Nancy Davies, who typed out text and captions far into the night;

The Syndics of the Fitzwilliam Museum, Cambridge;

Madeleine Ginsburg, friend and former colleague, for her active part in co-ordinating the different parts of this book, and her tact and understanding in so doing;

Michel Maignan for his help, expertise and for the loan of so many beautiful objects;

Marion Maule, who shared her fund of knowledge of the subject with enthusiasm and generosity of spirit;

John Salwey, for making available with great generosity, his grandmother's collection;

Ray Scott-White, former Master of the Worshipful Company of Fan Makers, for lending so many fine objects from his late father's collection;

The Rt. Hon. Bernard Weatherill M P for the precious loan of his most symbolic fan;

Other lenders: Margaret Lyons, Jacqueline Morris, Beryl Melville, Martin Willcocks and those who wish to remain anonymous for spontaneously coming forward with some of the most fascinating objects;

Also Anne Marie Benson of Phillips West Two, Marianne Harari, Yasuko Kido of Sotheby's, David Nash, Mr Ono, Cultural Attaché, Embassy of Japan, Mette Tang Simpson of Sotheby's, Susanna Watson of Harold Holt (The Japan Festival 1991);

Miranda Clarke for her careful and concise proof-reading;

Paula Hindley, Sophie Bishop and Gerald Ivall for their considerable contribution to the production of this volume;

Alan Tabor for his superb and imaginative photography of a very difficult subject;

Telford Shute and Paul Champkins for their support and encouragement from the concept to the completion;

and to the publisher, John Harrison-Banfield, for the fine design and presentation of this book.

Preface

The origins of this book lie in a sequence of events that began with the bold restoration of two Georgian houses, the future home of The Fan Museum, in Greenwich in 1987, and ended at the peak of the Japan Festival in late autumn of 1991 when *ŌGI – A History of the Japanese Fan* was published. In between, a group of individuals from every facet of the art world has combined to produce a remarkable book that covers, with new authority, a little written about aspect of Japanese decorative art, and that appears during an auspicious year for learning about Japan and things Japanese.

Representing the museum world is co-author Julia Hutt, a recognized authority on Far Eastern art and assistant curator at the Victoria and Albert Museum, London, who has previously written on Oriental fans, amongst other subjects. Mrs Hutt has contributed the historical section of this book. From the sphere of fan collecting and connoisseurship is the co-author, Hélène Alexander, whose remarkable dedication to the subject of this book has resulted in her founding The Fan Museum and assembling only their second exhibition 'Fans of the Four Seasons', which represents the latter part of the book and contains many examples from her own extensive collection.

Sponsoring this book are Spink & Son, London's oldest fine art dealers, who are joint publishers in association with the art publishers, Dauphin.

Finally, from the auctioneering world, is the retired head of Christie's Chinese and Japanese Department, and former senior diplomat in Japan, Sir John Figgess, KBE, CMG, who has kindly written the foreword.

Despite the profound efforts of those concerned, there is no doubt that the heart of this book is the fan itself. This elegant object with its multiplicity of purpose, from war to advertising, painter's canvas to assassin's weapon, fills the pages of this book with an extraordinary variety of colour, technique and design. *ŌGI* is a feast for those who have not yet discovered the art of the Japanese fan.

Paul Champkins
Director, Spink & Son Ltd, London
November 1991

Foreword

Japanese fans are familiar to everybody; indeed the fan is almost synonymous in most people's minds with Japan, and yet until the publication by Julia Hutt and Hélène Alexander of this well-researched history there was nowhere to turn to for accurate information on the origins, the variety and the truly vast scale of production of fans made in Japan both for the domestic market and, later, for export to the West. As the authors indicate, from very early times the decoration of the fan form appealed to some of the most celebrated Japanese artists whose fan paintings are preserved among their master works in Japanese collections. Understandably, few, if any, actual examples of such masterpieces reached the West during the great period of the bulk export of fans at the end of the nineteenth and early part of the twentieth centuries. The decoration of those predominantly mass-produced fans nevertheless reflected something of the Japanese artistic sense and conveyed to the Western populace at large a fair idea of Japanese aesthetics. It is no doubt the case that for European Impressionist painters like Monet and his friends, the first sight of Japanese wood-block prints brought a stunning awareness of the originality of Japanese art; but it was the wide availability of the inexpensive and charmingly decorated fans that spread a notion of the arts of Japan among the middle classes in the West. For the best of these exports were no mere cheap reproductions but were the products of craftsmen with a tradition of several generations of working in paper, wood, lacquer and other decorative arts essential to the paraphernalia of elegant Japanese living prior to the headlong rush towards Westernization after about 1860 which left them without a domestic demand for their skills.

It is fortunate therefore that Julia Hutt, who has established a reputation as a foremost scholar of Japanese decorative arts, should have turned her attention to the subject of fans and produced this timely history. Her section on the history of fans is an encyclopedia of information in which every aspect of the subject is covered. It provides exactly the information one requires in a straightforward readable manner, and the addition of a glossary is very helpful.

By a happy coincidence, the publication of this book chimes in with the exhibition 'Fans of the Four Seasons', The Fan Museum's first international loan exhibition, which is at present on public view and offers an opportunity to examine some rare examples of Japanese fans from the Hélène Alexander Collection. Mrs Alexander, co-author, has used many examples from the exhibition in the second part of this book which she ably uses to illustrate the history of the Japanese fan in East and West.

Sir John Figgess, KBE, CMG
November 1991

Contents

Chronology

The system used here is based on that found in the *Kondansha Encyclopaedia of Japan*.

Jōmon period *c.10,000BC-c.300BC*

Yayoi period *c.300BC-c.AD300*

Kofun period *c.300-mid 6th century*

Asuka period *mid 6th century-710*

Nara period *710-794*

Heian period *794-1185*

Kamakura period *1185-1333*

Muromachi period *1333-1568*

Momoyama period *1568-1600*

Edo period *1600-1868*

Modern period *1868-*

Meiji era *1868-1912*

Taishō era *1912-1926*

Shōwa era *1926-1989*

Heisei era *1989-*

The origins and history of the Japanese Fan – Julia Hutt

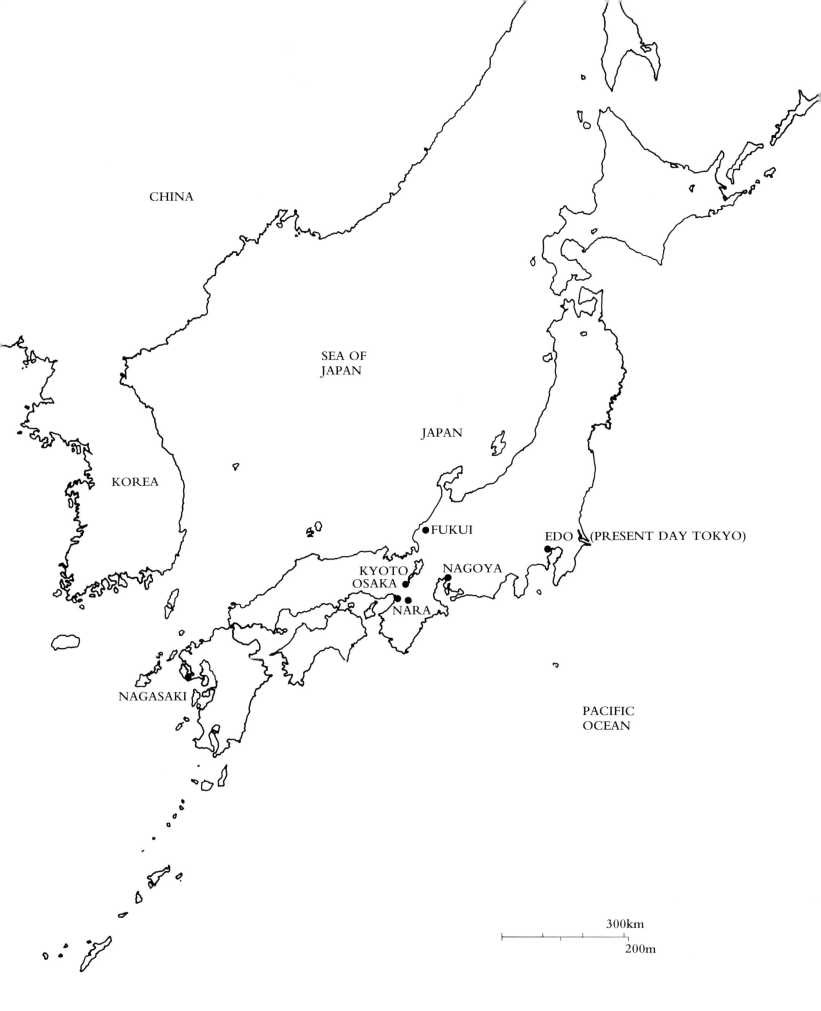

CHINA

SEA OF
JAPAN

KOREA

JAPAN

●FUKUI

EDO (PRESENT DAY TOKYO)
●

KYOTO NAGOYA
OSAKA ●
●
●NARA

NAGASAKI

PACIFIC
OCEAN

300km

200m

The origins and history of the Japanese Fan

In Japan, the importance of the fan went far beyond its use as an object with which to agitate the air and keep the bearer cool during the hot summer months. Over the course of its long history, the fan came to occupy an important role in many aspects of everyday life, as well as in court and religious circles, playing a vital role in the social intercourse and etiquette of Japan. Perhaps more than any other country of the world, the fan has come to be associated with Japan

Early History

Early Japanese history was closely connected with that of its culturally and technologically more advanced neighbour, China. With the introduction of Buddhism from China via Korea during the sixth century, came a wave of Chinese influence, reaching a peak during the Nara period (710-94). When official relations with China ceased after 894, there followed a period of introspection and assimilation of Chinese elements into most aspects of Japanese life, which resulted in the growth of a truly indigenous culture. Since the fan was used in China long before it first appeared in Japan, it is not surprising that early Japanese fans closely resemble those of the mainland. Early Chinese fans were of two types, namely the ceremonial fan, *tuan shan* ('round fan'), and the screen fan, *bian mian* ('screen fan').[1] The latter was any rigid fan which could conveniently be held in the hand. It was traditionally made of feathers or silk stretched over a round or oval frame. The ceremonial fan differed essentially in that it was of a larger size, was mounted on a long pole and was used by attendants in the ceremonial entourage of high officials at important functions or processions.

The earliest fans in Japan also appear to have been of the rigid ceremonial and screen type, known collectively in Japanese as *uchiwa* ('round fan'). The earliest representation of a fan in Japan is a painting in colour on an inner wall of a sixth century tomb at Wakamiya, Fukuoka prefecture (Plate 1). On either side of a scene containing a boat, waves, two horses and a human figure are large palm-shaped fans with stripes radiating from the point at which they are attached to long poles. Prior to the Tang dynasty (618-907) in China, tail feathers of the peacock and

pheasant were widely used in the manufacture of ceremonial fans and the radiating stripes on these Japanese examples were undoubtedly intended to represent feathers. Another early representation of a fan in Japan is found on the west wall of the Takamatsuzuka burial mound at Asuka, Nara prefecture, dating from the late seventh or early eighth century.[2] One of a group of court ladies is portrayed holding a screen fan, which appears to consist of silk stretched over a circular frame, and which is held on a central stick.

Probably the earliest surviving Japanese fan or fan-like object is one preserved in the Shōsōin, the imperial repository of the Emperor Shōmu's possessions given by his widow to the Tōdaiji Temple, Nara, in 756. The fan in question is referred to as a *shubi* and consists of a large quantity of animal hairs fixed between two vertical pieces of wood, which are attached to a stick. It bears a striking resemblance to a similar object found on the

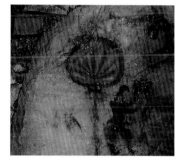

1. Painting in colour on the inner wall of the Takewara Tomb, Wakamiya, Fukuoka prefecture, depicting a boat, waves, two horses and a human figure flanked by a ceremonial fan on either side; sixth century. Reproduced from Genshoku Nihon No Bijutsu, *Vol. 1, published by Shogakukan, Tokyo, Japan.*

wall paintings of the cave-temple complex of Dunhuang, in northwest China, and was probably intended for ceremonial use or as a symbol of rank.

The Folding Fan

In both China and Japan, the folding fan was developed at an early date and, together with the rigid fan, formed the two basic fan formats used in East Asia. The early history of the folding fan remains unclear for it is not known with any certainty whether it was a Chinese or a Japanese invention, although circumstantial evidence points to the fact that it is quite likely to have originated in Japan. Even if it was invented in China, its subsequent development in Japan was such that even the Chinese attributed its invention to Japan.

In Japan, as in China, the invention of the folding fan was credited with some fanciful and imaginative origins. One of the most familiar stories, which exists in several versions, refers to a certain Toyomaru from Tamba province. Having been inspired by the anatomical shape of a bat's wing, which opens out fully and yet folds flat, he conceived of a fan which could be opened and folded up by means of sticks that moved about a fixed point. Another story credits the accidental invention of the folding fan to the widow of Taira Atsumori who retired to the Mieidō, a Kyoto temple. There she cured the abbot of a fever by uttering incantations and fanning him with a piece of paper folded into pleats. Such is the popularity of the story that many fan shops in Japan have traditionally been named 'Mieidō'. Apart from legends, there has also been some interesting research into the origins of the folding fan. According to the theory of Hiroko Yoshino, a scholar of folklore, for example, the folding fan derived from the use of the leaf of the *biro* palm, which spreads in the shape of a human hand, by female shamans in mystic rituals.[3]

Two types of folding fan were traditionally used in Japan, namely the *brisé* fan and the folding fan with a paper or silk leaf. Both types were unfolded when in use and then closed up again. The folding fan had a distinct advantage over the rigid fan as it could be folded up to a comparatively small size and placed inside a sleeve or in the folds of a *kimono* when not in use. The *brisé* fan consisted of flat strips of wood which were held together by means of a rivet at one end, while being connected together at the other end with ribbons or threads. The folding paper fan consisted of a number of thin sticks which were similarly held together by a rivet at one end, while the other end was held together by means of a single paper leaf which was pressed into folds.

The earliest literary references to the folding fan, in both Japan and China, date from the tenth century. A Japanese dictionary compiled around 935, for example, lists two types of fan, the *uchiwa* and the *ōgi*, the generic term for a folding fan. It is recorded in the *Song shu*, the official history of the Chinese Song dynasty (960-1279), that in 988 a Japanese monk, Chōnen, presented at court gifts of twelve *hiōgi* ('brisé fans') and two *kōmori ōgi* ('bat fans').[4] This would suggest that even if folding fans were not unknown in China, they still had sufficient novelty or rarity value to have been presented as gifts at court, together with the fact that they were obviously more widely available in Japan. There are also numerous references to folding fans in the great classical literature of the Heian period (794-1185), in particular the *Genji monogatari* (The tale of Genji) by Murasaki Shikibu and the *Makura no sōshi* (The pillow book) by Sei Shōnagon.

Already, by the end of the tenth century, the popularity of folding fans was such that sumptuary laws were promulgated during the Chōho era (999-1003) which restricted the decoration of both *hiōgi* and paper folding fans. In addition, a Chinese work of 1074 records that Korean embassies brought with them Japanese folding fans painted with birds, flowers and people.[5] Whereas folding fans were widely used in Japan from the 12th century onwards, it was not until the 15th century that the same was true of China. Although this does not rule out the fact that the folding fan originated in China rather than Japan this, together with other evidence such as mentioned above, would suggest that its origin lies in Japan. In either case, it was undoubtedly in Japan that the folding fan achieved a greater degree of popularity at a far earlier date. Moreover, under an entry for the year 1443, a Korean history of the Chosŏn dynasty (1392-1910) states that Japanese folding fans were exported to Korea and China in large numbers as Japanese specialities, along with swords and screens.[6]

The Court *Hiōgi* Fan

Whatever the origins of the folding fan, it is certain that one particular type of folding fan, the *brisé* or *hiōgi* fan, had no counterpart in China until the 18th century and was then almost exclusively confined to fans made for the Western market. The *hiōgi* derives its name from the fact that it was most frequently made from *hinoki* ('cypress wood'), thus *hi* refers to cypress and *ōgi* to fan (Plate 2). A widely accepted theory relating to the development of the *brisé* fan has been put forward by Kiyoe Nakamura, both a craftsman who has helped to preserve important fans, and a leading authority on the subject of Japanese fans.[7] He demonstrated the similarity between the *hiōgi* and *mokkan*, wooden tablets covered with writing which were used for a variety of administrative and commercial records by court officials of the Nara period. He also suggested that the next logical step would have been to string the slips together, either at one end or both, similar to a *brisé* fan. Indeed, a Buddhist image of Kannon, the bodhisattva of compassion and mercy, at the Tōji, a temple in Kyoto, was found to contain 20 wooden slips with inscriptions, one of which is dated 877. Although no rivet or thread was found, each slip reveals two holes at one end, which suggests that these may well have been threaded together at some stage. It is possible, therefore, that these 20 slips are an early *hiōgi* or that they represent a transitional stage between a *mokkan* and a *hiōgi* fan.[8]

Amongst the earliest surviving *hiōgi* are a number preserved in shrines at Itsukushima near Hiroshima, which date from the second half of the 12th century. These include three smaller fans which are traditionally associated with the boy emperor Antoku who died in a sea battle in 1185. The fans are made up of 34 or 35 blades of *hinoki* wood which taper towards the rivet end and which are connected with thread at the opposite end. The decorative surface of each fan is covered with *gofun*, powdered white lead, and on one example, it is also sprinkled with gold and silver powder. The fan face is painted with scenes typical of contemporary painting, frequently with courtiers amid trees and flowers.

The Japanese *hiōgi* in its fully developed form was the official court fan used for ceremonial purposes rather than for cooling oneself and it remained an item of court paraphernalia right through to the l9th century. Originally, only the emperor was permitted to use the *hiōgi* though, in time, it was used by all levels of the court aristocracy.

The *hiōgi* consists of a large number of wooden blades, usually between 34 and 38, held together with a metal rivet in the form of a butterfly on the front of the fan and a bird on the back. That of the empress, however, required a rivet made of paper string. At the other end, the blades were connected together by means of a silk cord. The fan face was painted in bright colours with carefully prescribed designs of pines, chrysanthemums, plum or cherry blossoms and, sometimes, birds on a white ground surrounded by stylized clouds in gold and silver, variously outlined in red, blue, green and purple. From the top of each guard hung clusters of artificial flowers and long silk cords of different colours. The overall effect of such a fan when fully open with court dress must have been stunning with its bright colours and long, flowing tassels. Although the designs of the fans and the colours of the cords to which various ranks of the nobility were entitled were regulated, these were not always strictly observed. For those under 16 years of age, a similar *hiōgi* was used but it was made of *sugi* ('cedar') instead of cypress wood.

2. Utagawa Kuniyoshi (1797-1861), A legendary court lady, woodblock colour print, c.1846-7. In accordance with the regulations of court dress, she is depicted with a hiōgi fan. Victoria and Albert Museum, London.

Folding Fans with Painted Leaves

Developing alongside the *hiōgi*, the folding fan with a paper leaf was extremely popular in Japan from at least the 12th century. Early paper folding fans consisted of a small number of wooden sticks, averaging between five and nine, which were held together with a single folded paper leaf. The end sticks were not differentiated to form guards at this early date and consisted of the same thin sticks. When fully opened, early folding fans were of a wedge shape, rarely opening beyond a ninety-degree spread. Since so few early paper folding fans have survived and since those that have are in such a poor state of preservation,[9] it is necessary to look beyond the fans themselves for information. One of the earliest representations of the paper folding fan in Japan is thought to be on an early tenth century wooden box for the storage of Buddhist sutras in the Tōji Temple. It is painted with Chinese figures playing a variety of games, two of the figures holding what appear to be closed folding fans.

It is, indeed, fortunate that the narrative style of painting which predominated during the late Heian and early Kamakura (1185-1333) periods frequently portrayed scenes of everyday life from all levels of society. Great emphasis was placed on the human figure, together with accessories and accoutrements of daily life, including the fan. Particularly informative with regard to depictions of the fan are the *Chōjū giga* (scroll of frolicking animals and people), the *Ban Dainagon emaki* (scroll of the story of the courtier Ban Dainagon), as well as the *Genji monogatari emaki* (scroll of the tale of Genji).[10] In some cases, the style of painting and the amount of detail are such as to depict the decoration on the fan itself while, in other cases, the depiction is extremely cursory. Nevertheless, it is abundantly clear from such paintings that, already by the end of the 12th century, decorated paper folding fans were in widespread use and far outnumber the few depictions of the rigid fan.

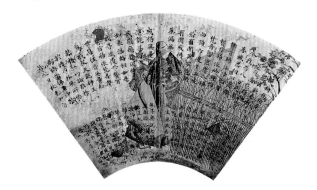

3. Sutra fan leaf, A lady holding a maple leaf, in ink and colour on decorated paper, over which is written part of the text of the Lotus Sutra; second half 12th century. Shitennōji Temple, Osaka.

Painted Sutra Fans

The earliest paper fans to have survived in significant numbers are painted sutra fans dating from the second half of the 12th century (Plate 3). The fans are remarkable in that they are painted with lively genre scenes over which texts from the Lotus Sutra are written. Since it was widely believed at the time that the end of the Buddhist Law was imminent, the Tendai sect of Buddhism, which was popular then, taught that salvation could be achieved through faith in the Buddha and in the teachings of the Lotus Sutra. This resulted in an increase in the building of temples, the manufacture of images and the copying of religious texts, particularly those of the Lotus Sutra. Although such texts are frequently decorated with painted scenes, such a combination of the religious and secular is rare, though it is also encountered in a few known sutras in book form. This use of the popular painted folding fan format together with an additional means of attempting to secure religious salvation is an interesting aspect of the history of the Japanese fan.

This group of sutra fans originally numbered 115 which, together, comprised the complete text of the Lotus Sutra. The fan leaves, like so many other scrolls of copied texts, consist of extremely fine quality paper decorated with gold and silver foil, which was cut into comparatively large squares or was finely powdered. The paper leaf is of a wedge shape which is comparatively deep from top to bottom when compared to later fan leaves. It is evident even from this early date that the artist was fully aware of the challenges offered by the fan shape. In some of the most successful and sophisticated fan paintings, the composition is not merely conceived in a rectangular form and then elongated or shortened to fit the fan shape, since elements of the composition, such as vertical or diagonal lines, the placing of a tree and so on, cleverly exploit the fan format to the full. In addition, the vertical columns of written characters fully take account of the fan shape, which is narrower at the base towards the rivet, so that the individual characters decrease in size accordingly towards the bottom of the leaf. There is no evidence as to whether the surviving paintings were ever actually mounted onto sticks and used as fans which, in any case, has undoubtedly contributed to their excellent state of preservation.

Folding Fans – Muromachi Period (1333–1568)
Surviving paper folding fans from the late Kamakura and Muromachi periods are few and far between. However, some information is provided by an unlikely source, namely the decoration of two lacquer toilet boxes, one in the Ōkura Shūkokan, Tokyo,[11] and the other in the Tokyo National Museum (Plate 4). The former dates from the early 14th century and the latter from a slightly later date. Both boxes are decorated with a design of open and closed folding fans, portrayed in considerable detail. Without exception, the fans all reveal landscape scenes. What is strikingly new, however, is that in the majority of cases the sticks have become thicker and more solid, while the two end sticks have become differentiated to form guards, which are decorated with pierced designs. Although there are still a few examples of fans with thin sticks and undifferentiated guards, the fact that the decorated guards predominate would suggest that this was the latest fashion during the 14th century.

4. Toilet box and cover with a design of scattered open and closed folding fans in gold togidashi, hiramakie, takamakie *and* nashiji; *14th century. Tokyo National Museum.*

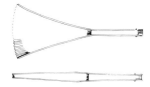

5. Drawing of closed suehiro *('wide-ended') and* bombori *('hand lantern') fans.*

Since the Muromachi was a period which witnessed a fresh wave of Chinese influence, it is hardly surprising that one of the main innovations to the Japanese folding fan during this period was of Chinese origin. From the outset, the Chinese folding fan had consisted of two semi-circular paper leaves, as opposed to one in Japan. In China, two identical leaves were pasted on either side of the sticks, which formed the support. From this period onwards in Japan, folding paper fans were manufactured with either a single or double sheet of folded paper, though the latter became the more common method of manufacture.

The 15th century also saw the appearance of the *suehiro* ('wide-ended') fan, which was used in court circles and by actors in the Noh theatre (Plate 5). This type of fan is characterized by a comparatively large number of sticks in relation to a fan leaf of short width, while the spread, when fully opened, does not exceed ninety degrees. The appearance of the fan when closed resembles that of a Y-shape, with the guards of the fan being splayed out, slightly pulling out the folds of the paper leaves. The sticks of such fans were usually of red or black lacquered wood and the guards pierced with a distinctive design, known as *nekome* ('cat's eyes'). Although the splayed appearance of the *suehiro* fan when closed initially came about due to technical problems in trying to accommodate the additional thickness of two fan leaves, the popularity of the shape of the fan resulted in the effect being produced deliberately. This was achieved either by using jointed guards or wood which could be made to splay out.

By contrast, another innovation of the Muromachi period was the *bombori* ('hand lantern') fan, which was an alternative method of dealing with the increased thickness of paper caused by using two paper leaves. Whereas the guards of the *suehiro* fan splayed out, those of the *bombori* curved sharply inwards, thus holding the pleated fan leaves firmly together.

Fan Painting
Painting was one of the most fundamental methods of decorating paper fans, employing the services of both amateur and professional painters. From the Muromachi period onwards, fan painting became an established and recognized branch of Japanese painting and many leading artists produced paintings for fans amongst their works (Plates 6-9). At the lower end of the market, painted fans could be bought ready mounted, whereas well-known artists frequently painted a fan leaf which was only mounted on sticks if required; some were never mounted. In the latter case, the challenge of conceiving and executing an appropriate design for the fan format was considered by the artist to be of paramount importance.

6. *Tani Bunchō (1763-1840)*, River and willows, *fan painting in ink on paper. Signed Bunchō, dated 1800. Bunchō was an artist of the Nanga school whose artists produced fan paintings as an important part of their work. British Museum, London.*

7. *Terutada Shikibu (early-mid 16th century)*, A mountain landscape, *fan painting in ink and gold on paper, with seals Terutada, Ryūkyō. British Museum, London.*

8. *Mori Sosen (1747-1821)*, Monkey by a shrub, *fan painting in ink and colour. Signed Sosen, with two seals (unread). Sosen is well known for his paintings of monkeys. Harari collection, Ashmolean Museum, Oxford.*

9. *Sakai Hōitsu (1761-1828)*, A branch of maple, *fan painting in ink and colour on a silver ground. Unsigned, with a seal Hōitsu. Hōitsu was an artist of the Rimpa school. Harari collection, Ashmolean Museum, Oxford.*

Indeed, both the artist and the person who commissioned or bought the fan leaf may have considered it far too precious to have it mounted as a fan, since the wear and tear on a paper leaf was considerable. The average fan had a short lifespan; most fans were bought at the beginning of the hot time of year and then discarded at the end of the season, if not before. Also, treasured fan leaves may have been removed from their sticks because of the fragility of the paper and thereby preserved for posterity by being mounted in an album, on a screen or as a hanging scroll. In other instances, an artist may have purchased ready made blank paper fans which he could then paint at will when the mood or occasion presented itself, such as to present to a friend as a record of an auspicious event. In addition, it is possible to ascertain whether a fan leaf was painted flat or after it was folded and mounted on sticks since, in the latter case, the ink or paint tended to 'pool' and was darker in tone along the vertical folds.

Tawaraya Sōtatsu and Ogata Kōrin

To discuss fan painting in greater depth would necessitate tracing the full development of Japanese painting. However, two artists deserve to be singled out for their special contribution to the development of fan painting as a separate category. Tawaraya Sōtatsu (died c. 1642) and Ogata Kōrin (1658-1716) were artists of exceptional talent who worked in highly individual and distinctive decorative styles of painting. Sōtatsu presided over a highly successful workshop in Kyoto which specialized in fan painting, while he was also the first named artist who can be associated with a large number of fan paintings. More than any artist before, Sōtatsu displayed a remarkable talent for relating his designs to the folding fan format. This can be seen in the way that the composition radiates from the centre of an imaginary circle, corresponding more or less with the rivet of the fan. So important was fan painting in Sōtatsu's formative years that this concept of design permeated many of his works in formats other than the fan leaf, especially the screen. In addition, he successfully achieved a degree of movement within the limited format, in the direction of right to left. It is interesting to note that this was the same direction as that of a handscroll which

was opened from left to right, like the fan, and viewed from right to left. Perhaps Sōtatsu's best surviving works in the fan format are those mounted onto screens (Plate 10) in the Samboin at the Daigoji, a temple in Kyoto, and in the Imperial Household Collection.

Ogata Kōrin greatly admired and respected the works of Sōtatsu and, although a man of great artistic talent in his own right, was undoubtedly indebted to him in many ways. Kōrin, like Sōtatsu, painted fan leaves though he preferred the rounded form of the rigid fan (Plate 11). Having been born into a family that owned a textile business, Kōrin was undoubtedly influenced by his early experimentation with circular compositions as kimono decoration. This predilection for circles and circular movement was ideally suited to the rigid fan format and may also be noticed in many of his compositions for other formats, such as the screen. Kōrin's intuitive feeling for format, medium and design is admirably exemplified by a gold lacquer box and cover in the Yamato Bunkakan, Nara, with both painted folding and round fans applied over the surface area, though not all the fans are thought to be by Kōrin's hand.[12]

Ukiyoe Prints and Printed Fan Leaves

The rise of Ukiyoe woodblock printing during the Edo period (1600-1868) proved an enormous impetus to the development of the fan in Japan. The Edo period was one of prolonged peace, which witnessed the rise of a wealthy merchant class, along with thriving urban centres, such as Edo (modern Tokyo) and Osaka. Since, owing to the rigid structure of Japanese society, merchants could not use their new-found wealth to improve their social status or to seek political power, they sought alternative outlets for their money, frequently in the pursuit of leisure activities and, materially, in the form of art objects. The newly developing Ukiyoe print, which portrayed scenes of everyday life, frequently centred on the Yoshiwara, the entertainment and pleasure quarters of Edo, with its licensed brothels, theatres, restaurants and tea houses. The Ukiyoe print did not rely wholly on any existing style of painting, and was something which the merchants and townspeople in general could easily understand and with

10. *Tawaraya Sōtatsu (died c.1642), six-fold screen with fan leaves painted in colour, gold and silver and pasted to a gold paper ground, together with a number of smaller paintings representing closed and partially open fans. Courtesy of the Freer Gallery of Art, Smithsonian Institution, Washington, D.C.*

12. *Probably by Hiroshige II (1826-69), The bay at Kuroto in Kazusa* province, *from a series of views of the provinces, woodblock colour print mounted on bamboo as an* uchiwa *fan. Signed Hiroshige ga, 1858. The Oriental Museum, Durham.*

11. *Ogata Kōrin (1658-1716), Narihira and the pilgrim, rigid fan painted in ink, gold and colour on paper over bamboo splints with a black lacquer handle. Courtesy of the Freer Gallery of Art, Smithsonian Institution, Washington, D.C.*

13. *Katsukawa Shunshō (1726-92) and Ippitsusai Bunchō (active c.1765-92), woodblock colour prints from* Ehon butai ōgi *(Picture book of the stage in fan shapes), published by Kariganeya Ihei, 3 vols., 1770. Victoria and Albert Museum, London.*

which they could readily identify. In terms of the fan, such printed fan leaves provided the mass of the population with cheap and fashionable substitutes for a painted fan leaf by one of the leading print designers of the day.

Printed fan leaves were produced in both the folding and rigid fan formats, though the latter tended to be the more popular. In some cases, it is evident that the print was never actually mounted as a fan while, in others, the fold lines indicate that it was used as a fan for a while before being removed from the sticks or frame and preserved. In yet other instances, a fan shape was used as an interesting device to frame the whole composition, though there may not have been any intention for the print to be mounted as a fan. One such example is the *Ehon butai ōgi* (Picture book of the stage in fan shapes) by Katsukawa Shunshō (1726-92) and Ippitsusai Bunchō (active c. 1765-92), published in three volumes in 1770 (Plate 13). This work is also of importance to the history of Ukiyoe prints in that the portraits depict individual actors for virtually the first time.

The rigid fan which was utilised by Ukiyoe print designers was of a type introduced from Korea at some time before the Edo period. Fans of this type consist of a piece of bamboo which was split down to a node or joint at a suitable point which would prevent any further splitting (Plate 12). The intact section of bamboo below the node formed the handle, while that above was split into numerous thin splints, usually between 50 and 60, of roughly equal thickness. These were splayed out in order to provide a firm base on which to paste a fan leaf on either side. Certain Ukiyoe print designers are particularly noted for their fan prints, notably Andō Hiroshige (1797-1858), Utagawa Kuniyoshi (1797-1861) and Utagawa Kunisada (1786-1864).

Just as the late Heian and Kamakura period narrative scrolls provide an excellent visual record of the development of fans during that time, so too do Ukiyoe prints provide an excellent record for their development during the Edo period. The subjects portrayed on Ukiyoe prints range from general scenes of everyday life, which frequently reveal a host of different types and designs of fans (Plate 14), to an elegant courtesan with the latest fashion in fans

14. *Kitagawa Utamaro (1753-1806)*, Women on the Ryōgoku Bridge, *woodblock colour print, three sheets from a set of six, published by Ōmiya Gonkurō, 1795-1800. British Museum, London.*

15. *Kitagawa Utamaro (1753-1806)*, The beauty Ohisa, *woodblock colour print published by Tsutaya Jūsaburō, c.1792-3. She holds a rigid fan which bears a* mon *(family crest). Sotheby's.* ▼

16. *Kitagawa Utamaro (1753-1806)*, The seller of fans, *woodblock colour print, 1795-1800. The fan seller carries several rigid fans by means of a pair of bamboo poles. British Museum, London.* ▶

21

(Plate 15), and the referee of a Sumo wrestling match holding his fan aloft, to itinerant fan sellers and the portrayal of fan shops, complete with craftsmen at work inside them. It is from this last type of print that it is possible to obtain information regarding the sale of fans during the latter part of the Edo period. In such retail outlets, it was possible to purchase ready mounted folding or rigid fans with painted or printed fan leaves. Alternatively, the customer could choose from a whole range of designs and have them made up with sticks or frames of his or her choice. Available designs were bound together in an album from which a choice could be made, while the sheets themselves were kept in boxes at the back of the shop.

Fans could also be obtained from street vendors who either bought them wholesale from retail outlets or who took them on a commission basis. Such vendors had the advantage of being able to reach a wider market, particularly at events of mass participation, such as the Kabuki theatre, where fans depicting the leading actors were often on sale. When such fan vendors were themselves the subject of Ukiyoe prints, it is interesting to observe the means they employed to carry around rigid fans: usually a pair of bamboo poles (Plate 16). Although the fans were relatively cumbersome, their extremely light weight made it possible to carry large quantities with comparative ease.

The fan had become firmly established as an essential item of daily use during the hot summer months through all levels of society by the Edo period, if not already long before. Whereas in the West social convention dictated that the fan was used almost exclusively by women, in Japan both men and women availed themselves of the fan. The poor made use of cheap and simple rigid fans of bamboo, while those with greater spending power bought more sophisticated folding or rigid fans which were mass-produced, individually painted or, more rarely, specially commissioned. Apart from the cheapest type of fan, the decorated rigid fan was almost exclusively used by women, whereas men tended to favour the folding fan. It was also customary for men to use fans which were sombre and restrained, some even plain white or undecorated.

The Fan in Everyday Life

During the course of its development in Japan, the uses to which the fan was put had proliferated, with particular types and designs evolving for specific occasions. In addition, certain manners and forms of etiquette had grown up around the fan. The open fan, for example, could conveniently be used to screen the face, so as to avoid protracted formal greeting, to hide embarrassment or to conceal the open mouth when laughing. In addition, since the kimono frequently had long, cumbersome sleeves, the fan could be used as a kind of extension of the hands to pass objects to another person. Fans were also exchanged with new acquaintances or as tokens of love. At night, during a firefly-hunting party, fans, particularly those of the uchiwa type, were used to stop the insects from settling and to agitate them into the air. It was also customary to celebrate various stages in a child's life, from birth through to coming of age, by dressing it in a splendid kimono and presenting it at the local shrine, complete with an appropriate auspicious fan. Similar celebrations and accompanying fans also took place when a person reached the age of 77 years.

There was even a game, known as tōsenkyo ('the pleasure of throwing a fan'), which involved a fan as its main constituent and which is thought to have been devised by a poet, Kisen, during the Ansei era (1772-80). It made use of a folding fan and a weighted target in the form of a leaf of a gingko tree, which is itself roughly fan-shaped. The object of the game was to take it in turns to throw a fan at the target and to knock it off a wooden stand, scoring according to how the target and fan fell on the floor. The game was initially popular amongst women and children of the leisured classes, though it gradually spread through all levels of society. The fact that it was an ideal gambling game, however, resulted in a series of prohibitions aimed at curbing this. At the height of its popularity, many books were published explaining its finer points, and the complexities of scoring. Another fan game involved floating a fan in water and composing a poem before the fan became completely submerged.

Military Fans

In the course of time, certain fans came to be associated with specific activities or events, frequently evolving distinctive forms, materials and decoration. Perhaps one of the best known examples was the *gunsen* ('war fan'), which was also known as the *tessen* ('iron fan'), and was used to give signals during battle. This was a folding fan composed of between 10 and 12 iron or lacquered wooden sticks with leaves of thick paper, decorated on one side with the red sun on a gold ground and on the other with a silver moon on a black ground. During the Edo period, a time of peace, *gunsen* were frequently made with black lacquered wooden sticks and ornamented metal guards as a decorative accessory for use with full armour on ceremonial occasions.

Related to the *gunsen* in use but not in appearance was the *gumpai uchiwa* ('military fan'). The *gumpai uchiwa* was a rigid fan made of iron and hardened leather or heavily lacquered wood with a handle which ran up to the top of the fan face. At the bottom end was a hole through which a thick cord was threaded, ending in a tassel. The fan was frequently decorated with the sun, moon and constellations of the stars. Like the *gunsen*, the main use of the *gumpai uchiwa* was as a baton for giving military commands but, on account of its form and material, it could also serve as a makeshift shield to parry blows or even as a weapon.

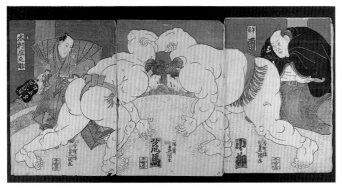

17. *Utagawa Kunisada (Utagawa Toyokuni III) (1786-1864),* Sumo wrestlers, *woodblock colour print in the triptych format, c.1847. On the left is the referee who holds a* gumpai uchiwa. *Victoria and Albert Museum, London.*

During the Edo period, the *gumpai uchiwa* was also intended for ceremonial or display purposes rather than for use in active warfare. A similar type of fan is used by the referee of a Sumo wrestling match as a symbol of his office (Plate 17). There was even a *tantō* ('dagger') fan which appeared to be an ordinary closed folding fan. In reality, however, it was a dagger and sheath in the form of a fan. This originally evolved as an ingenious way of concealing a potentially dangerous weapon by a would-be assassin. In time, however, the dagger 'fan' became important more for its novelty value than as a functional weapon. It has also been suggested that the *suehiro* ('wide-ended') fan developed expressly to avoid unscrupulous courtiers carrying around a dagger disguised as a fan. Although the true origins of the *suehiro* fan have already been discussed, it may also have been conveniently shaped to distinguish it at a glance from an ordinary closed folding fan of *bombori* shape (see Plate 5) and so discount the possible concealment of a dagger. A close examination of surviving *tantō* fans, however, reveals that they are a poor imitation of an actual closed fan which would not dupe anyone easily and, besides, a good craftsman would surely find a way to conceal a dagger in a *suehiro* fan shape if sufficiently determined.

Theatrical and Dance Fans

Fans played a prominent part in performances of the Noh and Kabuki theatres. Noh, the classical theatre of Japan, combines drama, song and dance. The leading actor, or actors, wears a lavish costume and an appropriate mask to personify the type of character he is portraying, while the whole performance is supported by the use of symbolic props, of which the fan is the most important. Since much of the spoken word in this type of theatre is unintelligible to the average Japanese, the fan is used by the actor to accentuate almost every gesture throughout the drama and to indicate to the audience, through manipulation and symbolic meaning, what is taking place. By positioning or moving the fan according to certain conventions, it can be used to indicate certain objects, actions or emotions. The fan is used in a similar manner during performances of

18. The actor Onoe Kikugorō VII as Shizuka Gozen from the play Yoshitsune senbon zakura *performed by the Kabukiza, Tokyo. Shizuka is using the fan to mime part of the plot. Contemporary photograph by Naotake Fukuda.*

19. Fan dancer, ink and colour on gold paper, 19th century in the style of the 17th century. British Museum, London.

FIG. 12.

20. Maki uchiwa *('roll fan'), women and child in boats, woodblock colour print. This illustration shows the fan both fully open and rolled up. From Charlotte Salwey,* Fans of Japan, *London, 1894.*

Kabuki, the popular theatre of Japan, which also combines acting and dancing (Plate 18). The type of fan commonly associated with the Noh and Kabuki theatre was the *maiōgi* ('dance fan'), a folding fan with approximately ten sticks and a thick paper leaf arranged in broad folds. However, different fans were used where appropriate, particularly in Kabuki, depending on the character portrayed and the context of the play. Theatrical fans are boldly and brightly painted, not only to add to the spectacle, but also to enable the audience to see their decoration from a distance and so to pick up any additional visual clues as to the events in the drama.

The fan was an integral part of dance in Japan, both in theatrical performances and as practised by ordinary dancing girls (Plate 19). Classical Japanese dance makes great use of the hands and arms rather than the legs and, in this way, the fan is used as an extension of the arms. It is a fundamental element of dance providing additional line, colour and shape. The theatrical *maiōgi* was the main type of fan to be used by dancers of all types and frequently included lead inserted into the guards or rivet to increase the weight of the fan and thereby facilitate flowing and graceful movement. One type of *maiōgi* consisted of a small number of thin sticks with either a pair of double guards or one guard split into two. The guards were attached to the fan leaf by means of silk cords which were secured in a criss-cross manner resembling lacing, being finished off at the upper end with small tassels. There was also a so-called 'fan dance' which was, in fact, more like a juggling performance than a dance, and which used fans as the essential prop. One by one, the performer built up the number of open folding fans he could carry by cleverly balancing them on his hands, feet, nose, mouth and forehead.

During the Edo period, the majority of fans were of the rigid type, ranging from simple bamboo fans, to printed fan leaves on a splayed bamboo frame and the more expensive silk or paper leaf stretched over a frame of a wide variety of shapes, including those of round, oval, almond, pear or fiddle-shaped outlines. In addition, a number of rigid fans evolved either for specific purposes or which display distinctive technical features of their manufacture. The

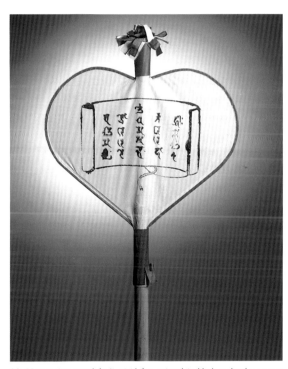

21. Mizu uchiwa *('water fan'), ducks, painted in colour on paper which was subsequently lacquered. From Charlotte Salwey,* Fans of Japan, *London, 1894.*

22. Hosen *('treasured fan'), rigid fan, printed in black and red on paper, with coloured streamers; contemporary. From the Tōshōdaiji Temple, Nara, where such fans are thrown by worshippers in the temple grounds on 19th May every year.*

shibu uchiwa ('persimmon juice fan'), for example, was used in the kitchen to revive the embers of a stove. It was made of bamboo covered with paper, which was then coated with the juice of the persimmon to give it additional strength and protection. Related to this was the *mizu uchiwa* ('water fan'), which was reputed to have originated in the town of Fukui, in Fukui prefecture (Plate 21). During hot weather, this type of fan could be dipped into cold water and, when agitated, the resulting process of evaporation helped to keep the bearer cool. In order to make the fan impermeable to water, it was dipped in oil and persimmon juice and, after drying, lacquered.

The *hamaguri uchiwa* ('clam fan') was a wooden fan, so called after its resemblance to the shape of a clam. Sometimes, the fan was made of silk stretched over a

wooden frame, in which case it was frequently embroidered on both sides. Of technical interest was the *maki uchiwa* ('roll fan'), ostensibly a rigid fan that could be rolled around the central stick, which also formed the handle, and tied with a cord (Plate 20). The circular fan face was inserted into a slot in the bamboo handle in such a way that it could revolve. When the bamboo splints of the fan face lay horizontal to the central stick, the fan could be secured fully open, and when the whole face was revolved so that the splints were vertical to the stick, the face could be rolled up and secured around it. The *mita ōgi* ('giant fan'), a type of cockade fan, was notable for its large size and form. The fan was constructed in such a way that, when opened, the large wooden sticks formed a circle, with a pair of guards forming the handles, which were considerably longer than the other sticks. This type of fan was traditionally used at the procession in honour of Amaterasu, the sun goddess, at the shrine of Ise, as well as in the procession of firemen.

Another type of fan was for use in the Tea Ceremony. It was known as *Rikyū ōgi* ('Rikyū fan') after Sen no Rikyū (1522-91), the greatest interpreter of the Tea Ceremony, who was said to have introduced it. This was a small folding fan, consisting of only three sticks with thick, strong paper and decorated in a restrained manner. However, such fans were not used for cooling the bearer but as 'plates' on which to serve guests with cakes.

The most important centres for the manufacture of fans were Edo (modern Tokyo), Osaka and Kyoto, though Nagoya, Yamato, Fushima, Fukui and Nara also produced certain varieties. Yamato, for example, was noted for a circular rigid fan which made use of transparent paper leaves. Inserted between the two leaves were figures which could only be seen when held up to the light. Nara, on the other hand, was famous for rigid fans which were composed of a stretched paper or silk fan face with perforated designs. The Tōshōdaiji Temple, Nara, is also well known for the *hosen* ('treasured fan'), a distinctive heart-shaped rigid fan, which is scattered by temple worshippers every year on 19th May, the anniversary of a certain priest's death (Plate 22).[13] The Gion Festival in Kyoto, a townspeople's festival which takes place on 17th July, is renowned for its use of fans which are carried by two men who stand in front of the floats.

23. Hotei, god of prosperity and one of the Seven Gods of Good Luck, holding a rigid fan; ivory netsuke with brown staining. Signed Kōhōsai (died c.1907), late 19th century. Victoria and Albert Museum, London.

The extent to which the fan is so deeply rooted in Japanese culture is reflected in the large number of myths and legends to have arisen which feature a fan as a vital element of the plot. One such story concerns the battle of Yashima in 1185 which ended a series of wars between the Taira and Minamoto clans (Plate 25). As a taunting challenge, Lady Tamamushi raised a folding fan bearing a sun motif on a pole at the head of one of the Taira boats. Since Juro, a skilled archer who had joined forces with the Minamoto clan, had hurt his arm, his brother, Yoichi, was called upon to shoot down the fan. He rode his horse well into the

24. Satsuma ware vase of baluster form. The sides are intricately decorated with two fan-shaped panels, 19th century. Spink & Son Ltd, London.

water, took aim and, according to legend, struck the rivet of the fan which then fell into the water. In addition, there are certain figures encountered in the repertoire of Japanese art whose main attribute is that of a fan. Hotei, for example, one of the Seven Gods of Good Luck, is portrayed as a jolly, balding man with an extremely large belly. He is invariably depicted with a sack and a distinctive rigid fan held in his hand (Plate 23).

As early as the 14th century, the fan appeared as a motif in its own right as the decoration on objects of art. Its earliest use seems to have been on three lacquer boxes, two of which have already been mentioned, and the fan has continued to be used as a motif for the decoration of lacquerware, particularly during the Edo period. Fans were also used to decorate metal *tsuba* ('sword guard'), as well as on the back, or non-reflective surface, of a bronze mirror, and are encountered extensively as a textile motif (Plate 26). In the field of ceramics, the folding fan shape was occasionally used to frame elements of the design (Plate 24), particularly on Imari-type porcelain, which was made for the export market from the late 17th century onwards. Objects made in the shape of both the rigid and the folding fan were also manufactured in lacquer, metal and pottery, usually in the form of a box and cover, or a dish.

The most important families in Japan traditionally made use of a *mon* or family crest as their insignia (Plate 27). This was used to mark family possessions, such as household utensils, and on formal *kimono*, as well as on the work

25. *Hideo Takeda (b. 1948),* Mark of the fan, *silkscreen, 1985. An irreverent reference to the fan incident in the wars between the Taira and Minamoto clans. British Museum, London.*

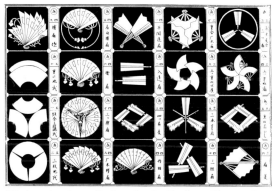

27. *A number of* mon *(family crest) each with a fan motif representing a different family.*

26. *Katsukawa Shunshō (1726-92),* The actor Yamashita Kintarō as Princess Usuyuki, *woodblock colour print c.1779. She wears a* kimono *with scattered* hiōgi *, fans, hairpins also in the form of* hiōgi *and a comb decorated with folding fans. Sotheby's.*

28. *Katsukawa Shunshō (1726-92),* A newly published brocade first night, *woodblock colour print in the form of a triptych. Outside a Kabuki theatre, two doormen each hold a folding fan which bears the* mon *of two leading actors in the play. British Museum, London.*

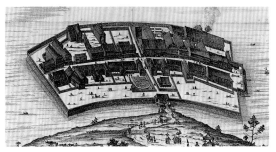

29. *View of Deshima Island, engraving, from Arnoldus Montanus,* Atlas Japonensis, *London, 1670 (English edition). The engraving clearly shows the layout of the Dutch Factory at Deshima. British Library, London.*

jackets of family retainers. In some instances, a *mon* consisted of a graphic stylization of an everyday object, such as a fan. Amongst over four thousand *mon* which were officially listed after the Meiji Restoration of 1868, there were many which took either the rigid or the folding fan as their motif, appearing in a wide variety of forms and combinations. The *mon* was sometimes used to decorate a fan, particularly that of a man, or it may have been used on a dancer's fan when she was employed by, or performing for, an important family. Prints showing a Kabuki theatre or a Sumo wrestling match sometimes also depict members of the audience holding a fan which bears the *mon* of their favourite actor or wrestler (Plate 28).

Fans for the Export Market

The Edo period, which lasted some 250 years, was not only a period of peace, but one of self-imposed isolation. By 1641, Japanese ships were forbidden to go abroad, while all foreigners were excluded from Japan, with the exception of Dutch and Chinese traders who were confined to the port of Nagasaki. In fact, their trading settlements were situated on the artificial, fan-shaped island of Deshima, which was connected to Nagasaki (Plate 29). The policy was rigidly enforced so that Japan was effectively closed to outside influences during the Edo period until the arrival of Commodore Matthew C. Perry's warships off Uraga Bay near Edo in 1853. In the following year, a treaty of friendship and commerce was concluded with the U.S.A. which opened up the ports of Hakodate and Shimoda to American ships for trade. Foreigners and outside influences slowly began to penetrate into Japan and, with the end of the Edo period and the imperial restoration of 1868, the floodgates were well and truly open. The Japanese were thus exposed to an influx of Western cultural influences and many foreign customs were adopted, including Western dress. By the same token, Japan was suddenly opened up to the outside world, and Westerners were made aware of a culture and its artefacts which had hitherto been virtually unknown. This resulted in an enormous vogue for anything connected with Japan and a Japan craze[14] seized Europe and the U.S.A. The average Westerner, however,

was more interested in acquiring Japanese objects of art than actually finding out about Japan and its people in any great depth.

As a result of the political and economic changes that took place during and immediately after the Meiji Restoration, large sections of the population were left relatively impoverished, which adversely affected their ability to purchase traditional arts and crafts. Coinciding with this, fortuitously, was the enormous demand for Japanese goods abroad; the Japanese craftsman responded accordingly, tailoring his traditional skills to what he thought the West wanted. The result was objects of art which Westerners considered to be wholly Japanese, but which could barely have been recognized as such by the Japanese themselves. It is against this background that the Japanese began to manufacture fans specifically for the export market.

Even before trade treaties were signed with individual Western nations, Japanese goods were exhibited on a small scale at various international exhibitions, such as those in London in 1851, New York in 1853 and Paris in 1855. It was the International Exhibition of 1862 in London, however, which for the first time exposed Westerners to Japanese art on a large scale. Sir Rutherford Alcock, the first British consul general in Japan, gathered together a collection of almost one thousand objects of Japanese

30. Souvenir postcard of a fan painter with folding and rigid fans, from one of the Japanese shops at the Japan-British Exhibition of 1910 at the White City, London. Private collection.

decorative arts which were exhibited at the Japanese Court of the London Exhibition. Other international exhibitions followed in Europe, while in America the Centennial Exhibition of 1876, which was held in Philadelphia, was produced on a grander scale than anything before. The type of objects exhibited included large quantities of Japanese metalwork, ceramics and lacquerware; although Japanese fans were fast becoming extremely popular, they were generally not considered sufficiently prestigious to be included, especially not in the early exhibitions (Plate 30). The Centennial Exhibition, however, included a separate Japanese bazaar which was expressly designed to sell more modest and affordable items, including both rigid and folding fans.[15] In addition, several different fans were produced to commemorate the exhibition, all of which were made in Japan. In the U.S.A., as in Europe, many exhibitions followed in other major cities.

During the last quarter of the 19th century, the fan remained an object of high fashion in the West. Chinese fans had been exported to the West since the early 18th century and, with the opening up of Japan, another country which was already skilled in their manufacture, it was a natural progression to obtain Japanese fans. If it was the great international exhibitions which exposed Westerners to the Japanese decorative arts, it was, for the most part, elsewhere that they needed to go to purchase Japanese fans. After the London Exhibition of 1862, many of the Japanese exhibits were purchased by Farmer and Rogers' Great Shawl and Cloak Emporium to form the basis of an oriental warehouse. One of the staff of two was Arthur Lasenby Liberty (1843-1917) who soon rose to the position of manager. Although Liberty had never been to Japan, he displayed an instinct for Japanese art objects and rapidly built the warehouse into a thriving business. In 1875, at the height of the Japanese craze, he branched out on his own and opened the modest East India House, which later became the famous Liberty's department store in Regent Street, London. It was in retail outlets such as these that Japanese fans could be bought.

The architect and designer, Edward W. Godwin (1833-86), having visited the London Exhibition of 1862, was a great admirer of Japanese art and a frequent visitor to East India House. In 1876 he wrote concerning the expected arrival of a new consignment of Japanese fans "There was quite a crowd when we arrived. A distinguished traveller had button-holed the obliging proprietor in one corner; a well known baronet, waiting to do the same, was trifling with some feather dusting brushes; two architects of well known names were posing an attendant in another corner with awkward questions; three distinguished painters with their wives blocked up the staircase; whilst a bevy of ladies filled up the rest of the floorspace.

"Before I could catch the eye of the master of this enchanting cave, it was learned that the cases would not arrive till late in the evening. Almost in a moment the swarm of folk vanished, and I was free to pick my way from ground-floor to attics, for No 218 Regent Street is from front to back and top to bottom literally crammed with objects of oriental manufacture."[16]

From an early date, Liberty's supplied silks and props for theatrical productions. During rehearsals for Gilbert and Sullivan's *The Mikado*, a light opera which opened on 14th March 1885, a reconstruction of a Japanese village was set up in Hyde Park.[17] Japanese personnel associated with the village were not only able to give practical help in designing costumes, props and scenery for *The Mikado*, but also instructed members of the cast in various Japanese ways and customs, including the correct usage of the fan. The enormous popularity of *The Mikado* led to the protagonists, the 'three little maids', being widely used to advertise the most mundane household goods in both Britain and the U.S.A., invariably clutching their fans.

At the height of their popularity, Japanese fans were exported in vast quantities. There are several contemporary sources that record the success of the trade, one of the best being J. J. Rein's *The Art Industries of Japan* published in 1889. Under the years 1881-85, he lists the total income from the export of Japanese fans, in yen, as 267,433, 156,854, 89,060, 94,992 and 107,945 respectively. For the year 1885, moreover, he also gives a break-down of the export of fans to different countries. The U.S.A. was by far the largest importer of Japanese fans, to the value of 79,558 yen, followed by France, England and Germany.[18] The fact that fans should have been listed at all is evidence of their great importance both as a source of revenue and in terms of their worldwide popularity. Another invaluable source is Charlotte M. Salwey's *Fans of Japan*, published in 1894, a work which, almost 100 years later, still remains one of the more scholarly and informative works on the subject. Salwey recorded separately the export of folding fans and rigid fans for the year 1890, with the U.S.A., Hong Kong, France and England, in that order, being the main purchasers. In 1891, the U.S.A. was again in the lead, followed this time by France, Hong Kong, China, and then England. The combined total of folding and rigid fans exported during the year 1891 reached the staggering total of 15,724,048.[19] The effect of this was perhaps inevitable. Already by 1876, Godwin wrote "Either the European market is ruining Japanese art or the Japanese have taken our artistic measure and found it wanting; perhaps there is a little of both. Take for example the common paper fan of today and compare it with some imported here ten or even eight years ago. Those are for the most part lovely in delicate colour and exquisite in drawing, but most of today's fans are impregnated with the crudeness of the European's sense of colour, and are immeasurably beneath the older examples."[20]

During the Japan craze, the fan was one of the cheapest Japanese objects available in the West and, for the average person, was possibly the only Japanese item they could hope to possess. In 1894, Salwey wrote "They [fans] find their way into almost every drawing-room and boudoir in our Western Hemisphere, and are twisted up with wool and silk and tawdry materials, and repainted by the modern Goth. They are set in fireplaces and windows as summer screens, put to all sorts of tortures, for letter-racks and tidies, and devoted to uses for which they were never intended."[21] This was a cry from the heart by someone who obviously loved the Japanese fan for its own sake and for its original purpose. In another section of the same book, Salwey comments "You may go into the homes of peasants who have spent all their lives in some out-of-the-way extremity of an obscure village, and find a Japanese fan in the ubiquitous corner cupboard."[22] This is echoed in Flora Thompson's *Lark Rise to Candleford,* an autobiographical work blended with a portrait of rural England around the turn of the century. In this book she wrote "The homes of these newly married couples illustrated a new phase in the hamlet's history . . . There were fancy touches hitherto unknown in the hamlet . . . Japanese fans appeared above picture frames and window curtains were tied back with ribbon bows."[23]

In China, fans made for the export market evolved a distinctive style which was quite separate from fans used by the Chinese. The same was true in Japan. Although Japanese export fans made use of traditional skills and materials, the end product was often quite new. A distinction should also be made between the mass of relatively cheap Japanese fans which flooded Western markets in their millions and the finer, more expensive examples. Of those that have survived, folding fans predominate though many of the cheaper varieties were probably of the rigid type. One of the most noticeable features of the folding fan made for the export market was the fact that it was comparatively large and opened up to a spread of roughly 180 degrees, and sometimes even more. In addition, new forms were introduced, such as the *cabriolet* fan which was made up of two or more concentric leaves, though they were strictly confined to the export fan. The materials used in the manufacture of export fans were also more varied and sumptuous than previously used in Japan. Whereas the *brisé* fan used by the Japanese, for example, was made of wood, those for the overseas market were more likely to have been made of ivory. Japanese taste, moreover, appreciated the inherent natural beauty of a material however simple, such as bamboo, particularly when contrasted with a decorated fan leaf.

As a general rule, the sticks of export fans became more ornate and elaborate. In the case of the folding paper fan, the sticks were usually made of wood or ivory, with small indentations on each side of the stick along its entire exposed length, while those used for the *brisé* fan frequently had ornate, curvy outlines. It was the fan guards, however, which were subject to the greatest change since, almost without exception, they became a focus of decorative attention (Plate 31). These varied from subtle carving, through gold lacquer on ivory, to ornate inlaid work, all of which may or may not have been of the

31. Fan guard (detail), with flowers and insects; ivory, incised and stained brown and encrusted with mother-of-pearl, tortoiseshell and hardstones.

same material as the rest of the fan.

Amongst the high quality fans for export is a group of ivory *brisé* fans decorated predominantly with gold lacquer in low and high relief, known as *hiramakie* ('low sprinkled picture') and *takamakie* ('high sprinkled picture') respectively. True lacquer is a sap obtained from the tree *rhus verniciflua*. After the lacquer is tapped and processed, successive layers are applied to a base material. After each layer has completely dried and hardened, it is polished smooth before adding the next layer, and the process is repeated many more times. Only after the numerous preparatory layers of lacquer are applied, can the master lacquerer begin to decorate the surface. Lacquer is coloured by the addition of vegetable and mineral dyes, including black, red, green and yellow. Gold or silver lacquer is obtained by combining metallic powders with transparent lacquer, the purity of the gold or silver varying considerably. The stages involved in making and decorating a lacquered object are thus highly complex and time-consuming, and lacquerwork remains an expensive craft. Since the lacquer industry was badly hit by economic conditions prevailing during the Meiji period (1868-1912), many traditional patrons could not afford to purchase lacquerware, which resulted in craftsmen turning their attention to the export market. Lacquer had been much sought after in Europe ever since it was first exported there during the late 16th century, with many attempts to produce artificial European substitutes. To produce ivory fans decorated with lacquer was thus an ideal solution to the problem. It was much quicker and, therefore, cheaper to concentrate on a relatively small area of decoration on an ivory fan, than to have to lacquer the base material and carry out the entire surface decoration as well. This resulted in high quality fans which were probably amongst the most expensive Japanese export fans. This is borne out by one source describing the Paris Exhibition of 1878 which states *"Ensuite vient le Japon avec des éventails brisés en bois et en ivoire ornés d'arabesques d'or ou d'insectes teintes et dorés. Les éventails sont en général assez riches et fort chers."*[24] They only appear to have been produced for a relatively short period of time and seem to have escaped the decline in quality so often associated with later export lacquer.[25]

Another distinctive type of fan decoration, which was used particularly for the guards, was the encrustation of an ivory or black lacquer ground with tiny pieces of material of various types. Work of this kind was commonly associated with the Shibayama family who had specialized in the decoration of lacquer *inrō* ('seal basket') since the late 18th century. The *inrō* was a small container composed of interlocking compartments, which was worn suspended from the *obi* (sash) by Japanese men and which became an object of great decorative attention (Plate 32). Shibayama workmanship was ideally suited to the small format of the *inrō*. It was characterized by minute pieces of inlay in a wide variety of materials, such as coral, tortoiseshell, ivory, bone and semi-precious stones, which were frequently intricately carved and applied to the base in such a way that they often stood out in relief (Plate 33). With the adoption of Western dress, the *inrō* largely fell from use and the many lacquer workshops which specialized in *inrō* decoration had to diversify. Shibayama-style decoration appealed greatly to European taste of the late 19th century though, under Western influence, it tended to become gaudy and fussy. As a general rule, however, when such decoration was applied to fans, it remained essentially restrained and was characterized, above all, by the portrayal of a wide variety of insects. It should also be remembered that although the Shibayama family made this type of inlay decoration popular, other craftsmen also worked in a similar style. Since few pieces are actually signed by a member of the Shibayama family, one should speak of 'Shibayama-style' rather than proved Shibayama workmanship in the absence of a signature.

It was not common practice to sign fans other than those painted by leading artists of the day. Such fan leaves were

32. Sheath inrō (detail of inner body), with design of folding fans in gold togidashi *on a black lacquer ground; second half 19th century. Spink & Son Ltd, London.*

33. Tray decorated with rigid fans and fan-shaped panels surrounded by hexagons, flowers and birds, in gold lacquer encrusted with shell, coral and hardstones; signed Shibayama; Meiji period (1868-1912). Spink & Son Ltd, London.

34. Claude Monet, La Japonaise, oil painting, 1876. 1951 Purchase Fund. Courtesy, Museum of Fine Arts, Boston, Massachusetts.

important first and foremost as paintings in the fan format rather than as fans. Everyday fans, for the most part, were not considered worthy of having a signature of the artist or craftsman added to them. The main exception to this, however, was the Ukiyoe fan print since the identity of the print designer was of paramount importance and they are, almost without exception, signed with his name. Fan leaves painted for the export market were not often signed or inscribed, since the majority were carried out by lesser known or unrecorded artists. In the West, moreover, at the end of the 19th century, any knowledge of Japanese was extremely rare and a fan was appreciated for factors other than its association with known Japanese artists.

The majority of fans for the export market evolved a style of decoration and choice of subject matter which was distinctive. There was an evident preference for people or things which Westerners considered as being Japanese, or associated with Japan. For example, depictions of Mount Fuji abound, together with figures in Japanese dress, in a manner reminiscent of Ukiyoe prints, and often in a landscape setting. Alternatively, highly decorative scenes from nature with birds and flowers were also extremely popular.

At the height of the Japanese craze, Japanese fans were exported in their millions. The enormous demand affected the traditional methods of manufacture of what was essentially a small-scale, home-based industry. The various stages became increasingly specialized in workshops, with different groups of craftsmen preparing the component parts and making up the finished article. The vast majority of export fans were mass-produced, printed fans, probably of the rigid *uchiwa* type. From an early date, the price of Japanese export fans became a matter of prime importance. Rein, for example, wrote in 1889 "The finest [folding fans] manufactured in former times for home demands cost scarcely 5 yen, while now they are made for foreign customers with mother of pearl and ivory decorations to cost three or four times that amount. The large majority of foreign customers care principally, however, for the cheapness of these wares, and the market is greatly influenced thereby. A hundred of the common sort of Uchiwa may be purchased in Osaka for from 1 to 2 yen,

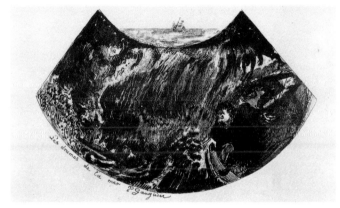

35. *Paul Gauguin (1848-1903),* Dramas of the Sea: a descent into the Maelstrom, *zincograph, 1889. National Gallery of Art, Washington, D.C.*

and singly, for from a halfpenny to a penny."[26] A year earlier, Marcus B. Huish wrote "An order for a million uchiwa shaped fans was recently placed in Japan at 800 dollars."[27] This incredibly low price implies that these must have been fans of a mass-produced variety. On the other hand, an American catalogue of circa 1800 from A. A. Vantine & Co., New York, describes a paper fan with a bright floral design available on a red, blue or silver ground with a lacquer handle as costing 8½ cents.[28] Such fans would appear to be from one of the middle price bands. What seems remarkable from such information is that the price differential of Japanese fans available on the market was relatively low and not commensurate with either the amount of work or the materials used in their manufacture.

It was in the field of advertising in its broadest sense that fans both for home consumption and for the export market shared a common ground. In both China and Japan during the 19th century, it was customary to produce printed fan leaves with topographical maps of an area. Apart from their limited practical use as maps, such fans also amounted to an early form of tourist advertising, as well as souvenirs. During the late 19th century, Japanese companies and establishments also used the fan, with printed leaves, as a highly successful form of cheap advertising. At the same time, Western restaurants, theatres and department stores, to mention a few, had similar advertising fans printed and made up in Japan for distribution to their customers and patrons abroad. This practice has continued in the 20th century and, even though the fan has long since ceased to be an object of fashion, such fans still have considerable novelty value today.

The enormous impact of Japanese art on that of the West and the subsequent rise of *Japonisme* is beyond the scope of this study. However, it is worth mentioning briefly that the influence of the Japanese fan on European art of the late 19th century is unmistakable. The majority of leading Impressionist painters, for example, painted scenes of Europeans surrounded by almost every conceivable Japanese art object, including the ubiquitous Ukiyoe print, as well as fans of the folding or rigid type. Perhaps the finest of these, *La Japonaise*, painted by Claude Monet in 1876, portrays a woman dressed in a sumptuous *kimono* holding a folding fan, while attached to the background wall and scattered on the floor are no less than 15 printed, rigid fans, each painted in remarkable detail (Plate 34). Many painters also experimented with the folding fan format, just as Japanese artists over the years sought to explore the possibilities for composition that it offered (Plate 35). And finally, amongst the various decorative arts, examples of the fan motif are endless, including both the folding and rigid fan shape.

In many countries of the world where it was once widely used both as a means of keeping oneself cool and as an object of high fashion, the fan has all but disappeared from use. In Japan, however, the fan has remained an item of everyday use down to the present day. The fan is not only a welcome accessory during the hot summer months, but the fact that it has a long history in Japan ensured that, over the course of time, it became an integral part of many facets of civil and ceremonial life. Even today, the fan may still be seen as an essential prop in the theatre, for example, or be used by the referee of a Sumo wrestling match. It is also used in certain Shinto and Buddhist ceremonies, and forms an essential part of various festivals. The manufacture of fans is still very much alive today, as both expensive one-off items and as mass-produced wares. Apart from the use of plastic for the frames of the cheaper fans, the techniques and materials employed remain little changed.

One of the chief characteristics of the Japanese climate is its distinct seasonal changes. This is reflected in the changing weather patterns, different plants which flourish at certain times of the year, as well as seasonal activities, such as planting the rice, and the depiction of various festivals. In the West, most people are familiar with the famous spring cherry blossoms and the chrysanthemums or maple trees of autumn, but there are many far more subtle allusions to the four seasons in Japan. It is extremely fitting, therefore, that the seasonal variations which result in hot summers and which have traditionally made the use of the fan so necessary, should also provide the subject for this exhibition of Japanese fans.

Julia Hutt

Footnotes

1. For a full discussion of the Chinese fan, see Hutt, Julia, 'Chinese fans and fans from China', *Fans from the East,* London, 1978, pp. 26-35.

2. This is illustrated in Ienaga, Saburo, *Painting in the Yamato style,* New York and Tokyo, 1973, p. 13, pl. 4.

3. Umehara, Munetaka, 'Multifacets of the Japanese fan', *Hilton Horizon,* Vol. 7, No. 2, Winter issue 1985, p. 12.

4. Earle, Joe 'The fan in Japan', *Fans from the East,* London, 1978, p. 38.

5. *Ibid.* p. 38.

6. Murase, Miyeko, *Byōbu, Japanese screens from a New York collection,* New York, 1971, p. 14.

7. Earle, *op. cit.,* p. 37, and Umehara, *op. cit.,* pp. 12-13.

8. Although the sticks of this particular *mokkan/hiōgi* are of dimensions more suited to a fan than a normal *mokkan,* they do not taper towards the rivet end as one would expect if they had been conceived as a *brisé* fan. In addition, since the writing does not extend from one stick to the next and is often partly obliterated by the adjoining stick, the writing was obviously added to individual sticks before they were joined together.

9. For a reference to one such fan see Earle, *op. cit.,* p. 38.

10. There are numerous illustrations from these scrolls in Ienaga, Saburo, *Painting in the Yamato style,* New York and Tokyo, 1973 and Hempel, Rose, *The Heian civilization of Japan,* Oxford, 1983.

11. The box in the Ōkura Shūkokan, Tokyo, is illustrated in von Ragué, Beatrix, *A history of Japanese lacquerwork,* Toronto and Buffalo, 1976, p. 80, pl. 62.

12. This is illustrated in Mizuo, Hiroshi, *Edo painting: Sōtatsu and Kōrin,* New York and Tokyo, 1972, pl. 78 and fig. 99.

13. I am very grateful to Marion Maule for bringing this type of fan to my attention.

14. The term 'Japan craze' was first used by the American Japanophile Edward S. Morse after the opening up of Japan.

15. The Japanese bazaar, complete with fans displayed on the rear wall, is illustrated in Hosley, William, *The Japan idea,* Hartford, Connecticut, 1990, Fig. 12, p. 36.

16. Adburgham, Alison, 'Taking Liberty's: the story of a London store and Japan', *Japan digest,* vol. 2, no. 1, July 1991, p. 56.

17. Pearse, Bowen, *Companion to Japanese Britain and Ireland,* Brighton, 1991, pp. 12-14.

18. Rein, J. J., *The Art Industries of Japan,* London, 1889, pp. 546-7.

19. Salwey, Charlotte M., *Fans of Japan,* London, 1894, pp 133-5

20. Adburgham, *op. cit.,* p. 56.

21. Salwey, *op. cit.,* p. 47.

22. *Ibid.* p. 131.

23. Thompson, Flora, *Lark Rise to Candleford,* Harmondsworth, Middlesex, 1974, p. 171. I am very grateful to Marion Maule for bringing this reference to my attention.

24. Lacroix, E., *Études sur l'exposition de 1878,* Paris, 1878, vol. 7, p. 77. I am very grateful to Madeleine Ginsburg for searching through literature on the international exhibitions for this information.

25. Wooliscroft Rhead, G., *History of the fan,* London, 1910, pp. 74-5, mentions 'The excellent example in the Victoria and Albert Museum is decorated with circular medallions in gold lacquer of various shades, portions being carved in relief. It is finely inlaid in places with mother of pearl; signed by Taishin (a pupil of Zeshin), and dated 1884.' Unfortunately, no such fan can be found in the collection of the V&A. Although it is quite feasible that the well-known lacquerer Ikeda Taishin (1825-1903) carried out such a fan in 1884, this cannot be verified.

26. Rein, *op. cit.,* p. 416.

27. Huish, Marcus B., *Japan and its art,* London, 1888, p. 91.

28. Hosley, *op. cit.,* p. 204, end-notes no. 116.

The Fan Museum and a selection of fans from the exhibition

FANS OF THE FOUR SEASONS

The Fan Museum, Greenwich

Fans, like other decorative objects, relate to both the culture and style of their owners. These intimate or functional items are usually on a small scale. It is therefore fitting that they be displayed in an elegant domestic setting and The Fan Museum in London provides the perfect solution. Thanks to a herculean effort on the part of The Fan Museum Trust, the Museum's governing body, two early Georgian town houses (1721) have been lovingly and painstakingly restored and adapted to the very special needs of the Museum. This major enterprise was begun in 1985 and completed in the spring of 1991.

The Fan Museum's prime objective is to bring the fan to the attention of an ever wider public, by showing it as something which touches upon every aspect of social life and thus dispelling the frivolous image which this object, by its very nature, has tended to have. To this end, and also for reasons of conservation, the policy of the Museum is to hold thematic exhibitions which last up to four months. Eventually, this continuing series will allow all the 2,000 fans in the collection to be on display by rotation.

Fans and fan leaves which find a permanent or temporary home in The Fan Museum are given proper care and attention at all times. The importance of security is highlighted whilst the conditions under which the objects are kept and displayed are the result of continuous study and are regularly monitored. Levels of the light are controlled by the use of ultra-violet filters on the windows and fibre optics lighting is fixed into the permanent glass-display cases, which are specially designed to allow maximum flexibility for the change-over of displays. When not on display, the objects are stored in the Study Room which doubles as a library and archive. The Study Room's storage units are almost works of art in their own right with their strong but elegant design by Robin Williams, an artist working in wood in the West Country. A massive table with a banding of silver occupies the centre of the room which is truly the 'heart' of the building. Despite the attention given to modern technology, this remains a traditional museum, without being a 'stuffy' unnatural place of learning. It seeks to be, and to a great extent succeeds in being, one of those rare places where beauty and culture combine with elegant comfort and period charm: "*Là tout n'est qu'ordre et beauté, luxe, calme et volupté...*".

The Museum's fast-establishing standing within the academic world allows for the possibility of future international loan exhibitions, drawn from other establishments of culture, for, without a doubt, this is the first museum in the world devoted solely to fans. Whilst the first exhibition explored the theme of childhood in fans, the second seeks pastures new in presenting an exhibition of fans from Japan: 'Fans of the Four Seasons', which coincided with the nationwide Festival of Japan in 1991. It would not be an exaggeration to suggest that The Fan Museum aspires to an order of excellence in everything that it undertakes, and the quality of the exhibition underlines this aim.

During the late 19th century, a Japanese exhibition was held in Knightsbridge in London. Japanese women involved in the event were employed by Gilbert (of light opera fame) to teach the members of the cast of *The Mikado* how to walk, use a fan, dress, etc. in the Japanese manner. Through this association, links were forged which led to many more friendly exchanges. These moments of history are recorded on fans such as no. 65 which is decorated with the flag of Japan and the White Ensign (The Royal Navy) entwined. This fan also reminds us of a past, more gracious era when the fan was an important accessory to European women, as it continues to be today to their Japanese counterparts.

The Fan Museum is related to one of the most important collections of Japanese art, the collection of the late Ralph Harari which comprises, among its treasures, a fan leaf mentioned in the *Journal des Goncourt*.

Ralph Harari was a first cousin of Marie Adda, the author's mother. He shared a love and enthusiasm for Japanese art with the author's father, Victor Adda, who was an eminent collector and connoisseur and the inspiration for The Fan Museum.

The exhibits in the 'Fans of the Four Seasons' are, in the main, from private collections and they have been carefully assembled to give a general view of the traditional fans of Japan, as well as those made specifically for export. The collection also includes contemporary Japanese examples. However, the heart of the exhibition comprises the fans of

Charlotte Salwey, the pioneering author of *Fans of Japan*, 1894. It was by pure chance that her fans came to light for they had not been seen since Mrs Salwey wrote her book, which remains one of the most authoritative on the subject. Her grandson, Mr John Salwey, has lent the re-discovered Salwey fans to the Museum and his kindness and generosity can only be matched by that of the loans from the Rt. Hon. Bernard Weatherill, Speaker of the House of Commons, and Mr Ray Scott-White, past Master of the Worshipful Company of Fan-Makers, whose father had been an engineer working in Tokyo in the 1920s and whose taste and foresight prompted him to collect *objets d'art* from Japan.

The Paris Exhibition of 1878 certainly crystallised the fan, in the eyes of an interested public, as a graceful object which had influenced European design since the early 1860s. Writing in 1879, Augustus Sala in his book *Paris Herself Again* states that, "on the whole, the surveys of those exhibitors' stands devoted to decorative furniture induce the conviction that the rage for the Japanese style has, in France at least, reached its climax". Despite his lack of attention to the decorative arts of other countries, he devotes over 500 pages to describing the exhibits from Great Britain and the way in which their decoration was influenced by Japan: "Mr R. W. Binns, the Director of the Worcester Porcelain Works, wisely indifferent to all crazes and fevers of fashion, has discriminatingly applied the truths which the Japanese models teach, with the result

that is much to be commended. Among examples exhibited, there are services as well as isolated pieces in which flowers and birds, treated after the Japanese fashion, are intermingled with butterflies and similar objects in gold and bronze relief, securing by this means a rich and solid effect very far superior to that of ordinary gilding . . .". There is also a chapter on the exhibition's gold medallists but, sadly, Mr Sala does not give credit to the winner in the Fan Class, the *eventailliste*, Duvelleroy, whose descendant, Mr Maignan, has not only lent fans and other fan-related objects, but has also lent his expertise in advising and assisting the working committee of this exhibition. No exhibition of Japanese fans would be complete without at least one example from the Rosse-Messel Collection. The Syndics of the Fitzwilliam Museum have most graciously agreed to lend one exhibit from this famous collection, no. 10, the superb *gumpai uchiwa*.

There are also anonymous lenders whose praises must be sung, for theirs is a selfless and totally disinterested contribution which is of the utmost importance in providing a varied and colourful display. The Fan Museum is not insensitive to the many debts of gratitude it owes to so many individuals and institutions which support it and it has always been the hope of the founders that some of these debts may be repaid by creating at the Museum not only an atmosphere of learning and quality, but one that is also coupled with helpfulness and enthusiasm.

Hélène Alexander

Traditional Japanese Fans

1 Fan Leaf

Date: Late 17th–early 18th century

A paper fan leaf painted with three courtiers in colour on a gold-flecked ground in the style of the Kanō school. An attendant holds a canopy over an important person while a third carries a staff of twisted wood. The fact that the leaf reveals fold marks and signs of wear and tear suggests that it was once mounted on sticks and used as a fan.

Width   50cm

Provenance: The Fan Museum, Hélène Alexander Collection.

Exhibition Number: 1

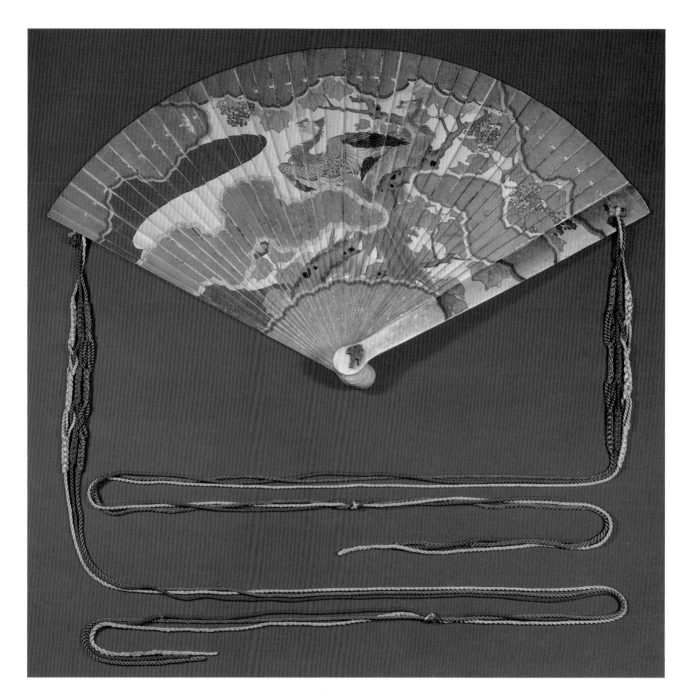

2 *Brisé* Fan

Date: 18th century

A *hiōgi* ('cypress fan'), made from cypress wood
which is painted white, and overpainted in bold
colours with two phoenixes on the branch of a
flowering tree surrounded by stylized clouds. The
reverse is painted with butterflies, birds and
stylized clouds. Attached to each *guard* are three
long silk *cords* of red, green and cream. The *rivet*
is made from metal and has a butterfly on one
side, and a bird on the other.
The *hiōgi* was the official court fan of Japan. (See
p.14 for a fuller description.)

Total height   39cm
Width   63cm

Provenance: Lent by Michel Maignan, Duvelleroy, Paris.

Exhibition Number: 3

References: For similar examples see *Fans from the East*,
London, 1978, p.11, pl.5 and Iröns, John Neville, *Fans of
Imperial Japan*, Hong Kong, 1981, p.83, pl.7.

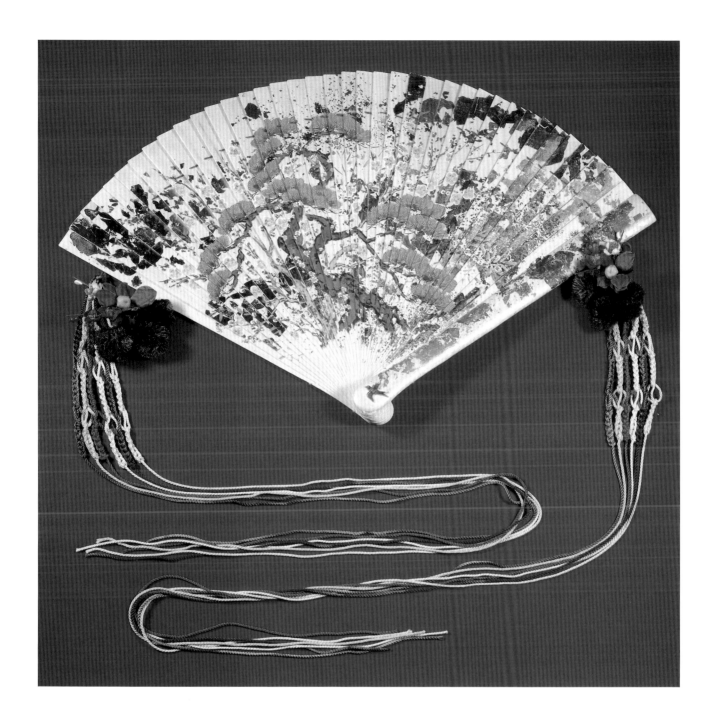

3 *Brisé* Fan
Date: 19th century

A *hiōgi* ('cypress fan'), made from cypress wood,
which is painted white and overpainted in bold
colours, though large areas of the paint have
flaked off. One face of the fan depicts a pine tree
and another tree in blossom while the *reverse*
portrays butterflies against gold and silver stylized
clouds. Attached to each *guard* are a bunch of
artificial flowers and six long coloured silk *cords*.

Total height   38cm
Width   61cm

Anonymous loan.

Exhibition Number: 4

References: For similar examples see *Fans from the East*,
London, 1978, p.11, pl.5 and Iröns, John Neville, *Fans of
Imperial Japan*, Hong Kong, 1981, p.83, pl.7.

4 Folding Fan
Date: Second half 19th century

A double paper leaf painted with a Japanese figure on the back of a crane flying over the sea on a blue and gold ground. The *reverse* portrays a Chinese figure on the back of a long-haired tortoise. Black lacquered *sticks* and *guards*, the latter with pierced *nekome* ('cat's eyes') designs. This is an example of a *suehiro* ('wide-ended') fan which looks as though it is partially open when it is actually closed. This fan has an ivory *rivet*.

Total height   32cm
Width   45cm

Provenance: Lent by Michel Maignan, Duvelleroy, Paris.

Exhibition Number: 5

5 Folding Fan
Date: Second half 19th century

A double paper leaf with roundels of flowers from the different seasons of the year painted in colours on a red and gold ground on one side, and red and silver on the other. Black lacquered *sticks* and *guards*, the latter with pierced *nekome* ('cat's eyes') designs. This is an example of a *suehiro* ('wide-ended') fan. The fan has its own shaped wooden box lined with silk.

Total height   34cm
Width   44cm

Provenance: Lent by Michel Maignan, Duvelleroy, Paris.

Exhibition Number: 6

Reference: Illustrated in Maignan, Michel, '*Oji & uchiwa*', Bulletin association Franco-Japonaise, Paris, No.18, October 1987, p.6, pl.8.

6 Folding Fan
Date: Second half 19th century

A double paper leaf with the 'Three Friends',
namely pine, bamboo and prunus, painted in
colours on a gold ground. Bamboo *sticks* and
guards, the latter with pierced *nekome* ('cat's eyes')
designs. This is an example of a *suehiro* ('wide-
ended') fan. The fan has a wooden *rivet*.

Total height	29.5cm
Width	54cm

Anonymous loan.

Exhibition Number: 7

7 Folding Fan
Date: Early 20th century

A double paper leaf with courtiers seated under a
pine tree and a flowering plant by a pond,
painted in colours on a red and gold ground. The
reverse depicts cranes in flight against clouds. Red
lacquered *sticks* and *guards*, the latter with pierced
nekome ('cat's eyes') designs. The fan has an ivory
rivet. This is an example of a *suehiro* ('wide-
ended') fan.

Total height	30cm
Width	42.5cm

Provenance: The Fan Museum, Hélène Alexander Collection.

Exhibition Number: 8

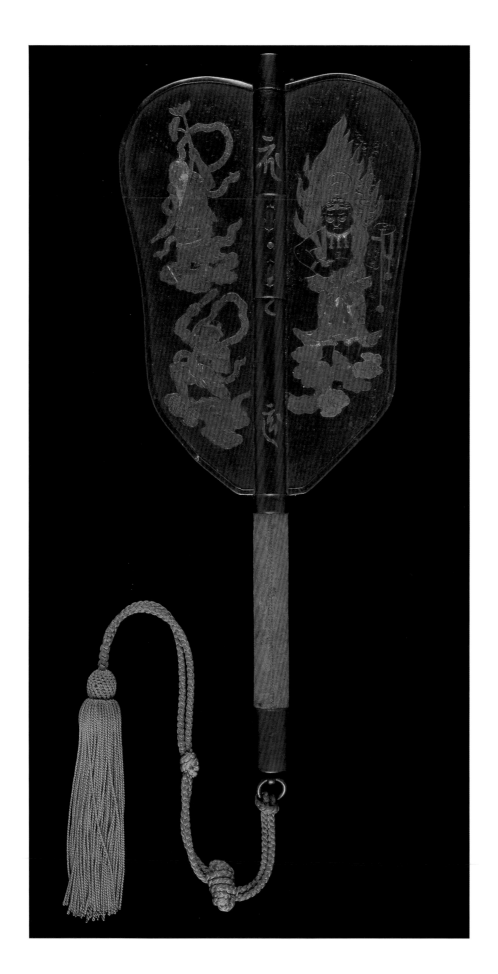

8 Fixed Fan
Date: 17th century

A *gumpai uchiwa*, or fixed iron fan, decorated with the sun and the moon in clouds with Sanskrit characters. The *reverse* shows Fudo Myō-ō and his attendants Seitaka and Kongara riding on clouds, with Sanskrit characters. The handle depicts a scrolling dragon and the rim is of iron. The stick is of wood covered in painted suede and iron. The fan has a *cord* and *tassel*.

Total height   44.2cm
Width   19cm

Provenance: Formerly in the collection of Colonel Leonard Messel (1872-1953) and Anne, Countess of Rosse. Purchased with a grant from the National Heritage Memorial Fund and a gift from the Friends of the Fitzwilliam.

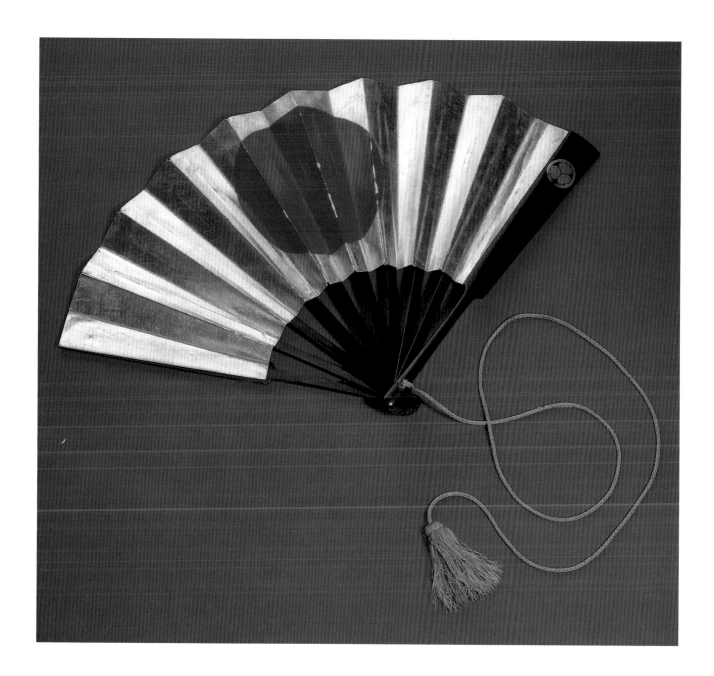

9 Folding Fan
Date: Second half 19th century

A double leaf of stiff red paper painted with a red circle, representing the sun, on a gold background. The *reverse* with a gold circle on a red background. Black lacquered wooden *sticks* and black lacquered iron *guards*, the latter bearing the Tokugawa *mon* (family crest) of three hollyhock leaves in gold *hiramakie*. This is an example of a *gunsen* ('war fan'). (See p.23 for a fuller description of this type of fan.) The fan has a metal *rivet* and long silk *cord* with matching *tassel* which is wound round the *guards* when the fan is closed.

| Total length | 33cm |
| Width | 53cm |

Provenance: The Fan Museum, Hélène Alexander Collection.

Exhibition Number: 10

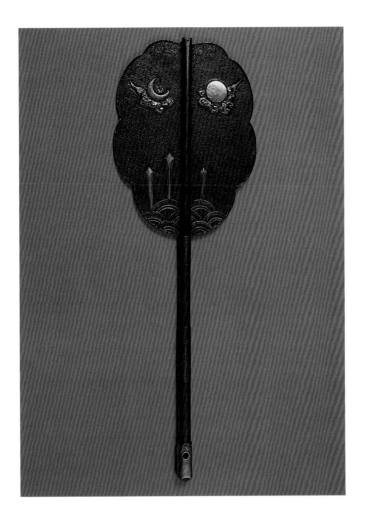

10 Fixed Fan
Date: 17th century

A *gumpai uchiwa*, or fixed iron fan, chased in low relief with gold and silver inlay. The handle is also made of iron, split and bound with iron wire with a silver ferule. It is decorated with the sun and the moon in conventional waves and rocks; the *reverse* shows the Polaris constellation over waves.

Total height   25.7cm
Width   8.6cm

Provenance: Formerly in the collection of Colonel Leonard Messel (1872-1953) and Anne, Countess of Rosse. Purchased with a grant from the National Heritage Memorial Fund and a gift from the Friends of the Fitzwilliam Museum. Lent by the Syndics of the Fitzwilliam Museum.

Exhibition Number: 9

11 Dagger Fan
Date: Second half 19th century

A metal dagger (*tantō*) and sheath of painted wood which is in the form of a closed folding fan. The 'fan' separates into two parts and, when pulled apart, reveals a sharp blade with the smaller part forming the handle. The dagger fan originally evolved as an ingenious way to conceal about the body a potentially dangerous weapon.

Length   30cm

Provenance: The Fan Museum, Hélène Alexander Collection.

Exhibition Number: 11

12 Folding Fan
Date: 19th century

A double paper leaf painted on both sides in black, brown and white on a silver ground with birds flying amongst foliage on a moonlit night. When held up to the light, the full moon appears translucent. Bamboo *sticks* and *guards*, with each guard split and splayed into two and attached to the leaf by means of silk *cords*. These are secured in a criss-cross manner and finished at the upper end with small *tassels*. This is an example of a *maiōgi* ('dance fan').

Total height   24cm
Width   60cm

Provenance: Formerly in the collection of Charlotte Salwey. Lent by John Salwey.

Exhibition Number: 14

13 Folding Fan
Date: 19th century

A double paper leaf with red-
and blue-tipped hibiscus flowers
painted in white, pink, blue,
yellow, red and orange on a
gold ground. The *reverse* is
painted with maple branches.
Bamboo *sticks* and *guards*, with
each guard split and splayed into
two and attached to the leaf by
means of silk *cords*. These are
secured in a criss-cross manner
and finished at the upper end
with small *tassels*. This is an
example of a *maiōgi* ('dance fan').

Total height   24cm
Width   60cm

Provenance: The Fan Museum, Hélène
Alexander Collection.

Exhibition Number: 15

14 Folding Fan
Date: Late 19th century

A double paper leaf painted on both sides with
irises in blue, green, pink and white on a gold
ground and with stylised waves in the
background. Bamboo *sticks* and *guards* with the
lead insert visible near the rivet. The fan has a
bamboo wedge *rivet*. This is an example of a
maiōgi ('dance fan').

Total length   28.5cm
Width   49.5cm

Anonymous loan.

Exhibition Number: 16

51

15 Folding Fan
Date: Late 19th century

A double paper leaf painted in red, white and black on a silver background. One side depicts a crane with outstretched wings flying over the waves of the sea, with a huge rising or setting sun behind. The *reverse* portrays cranes in flight on a gold-flecked ground. Black lacquered *sticks* and *guards*, with the lead insert visible near the *rivet*. Each guard is attached to the leaf by means of silk *cords* which are secured in a criss-cross manner. This is an example of a *maiōgi* ('dance fan').

Total height	29cm
Width	46.5cm

Provenance: The Fan Museum, Hélène Alexander Collection.

Exhibition Number: 17

16 Folding Fan
Date: Late 19th century

A double paper leaf covered with silk gauze and painted with pale green leaves on a yellow background. Bamboo *sticks* and *guards*, with each guard split into two and attached to the leaf by means of silk cords. These are secured in a criss-cross manner and are finished at the upper end with small *tassels*. The fan has a metal *loop* and *rivet*, with a silk *cord* and *tassel*.

Total height	33cm
Width	56cm

Provenance: Formerly in the collection of Charlotte Salwey. Lent by John Salwey.

Exhibition Number: 18

17 Fixed Fan
Date: Ryūkyū Islands, 19th century

A red and black lacquered wooden fan decorated with raised gold lacquer and two slatted apertures. On one side, three children are portrayed by a stream, with trees and a building. The *reverse* with two stylized characters (unread) and squares of mother-of-pearl in a chequered design. The fan also has shaped cartouches along the central pole which simulate metal attachments of the fan to the handle. This was probably used as a ceremonial fan. The Ryūkyū Islands, which are today part of Japan, have in turn been occupied by the Chinese and the Japanese, and artefacts from these islands reflect the styles and customs of both civilisations.

Fan face	25.5cm x 22.8cm
Handle	45cm

Provenance: Lent by Michel Maignan, Duvelleroy, Paris.

Exhibition Number: 19

References. Illustrated in Maignan, Michel, '*Oji & uchiwa*', Bulletin association Franco-Japonaise, Paris, No.18, October 1987, p.4, pl.1. For a similar example, see Jonathon Bourne et al, *Lacquer, an international history and collector's guide*, Crowood Press, 1984, p.139. Also illustrated in *Chinese and associated lacquer from the Garner Collection*, The British Museum, London, 1973, no.183, pl.79a. There is also a similar example in the Victoria and Albert Museum, London, no. W. 23-1919.

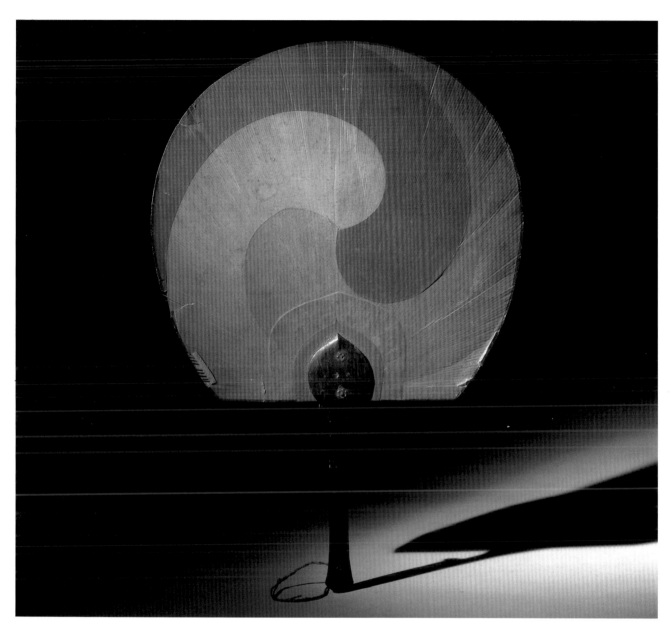

18 Fixed Fan
Date: Korean, last quarter 19th century

A fixed fan made of thin bamboo splints which are splayed out and secured round the edges. Coloured paper was then pasted on to the splints to form the two faces of the fan, which are decorated with the Korean *taegŭk* motif. The *taegŭk* is the Korean equivalent of the Chinese *tai ji* ('great ultimate'), which is commonly referred to as the *yin yang* symbol. Black lacquered handle.

Although this fan is Korean rather than Japanese, it is the classic Korean type which provided the model for Japanese *uchiwa* of the Edo period.

Total height   32cm
Width   23.8cm

Provenance: Formerly in the collection of Professor William Anderson, Chairman of the Council of the Japan Society in 1894. Lent by John Salwey.

Exhibition Number: 20

Reference: Illustrated in Salwey, Charlotte M., *Fans of Japan*, London, 1894, pl.1.

19 *Brisé* Fan
Date: Second half 19th century

The *sticks* are made up of five different types of wood, grouped together in batches of four, including the *guards*. Each face of the fan is decorated with gold and silver *hiramakie*, which has rubbed through in places to reveal black lacquer beneath. One side of the fan portrays a branch with leaves and berries while the *reverse* depicts a similar branch with fruit. The *guards* are decorated with pinks in gold *hiramakie*. The fan has a metal *rivet*.

Total height	23.5cm
Width	39cm

Provenance: Lent by Michel Maignan, Duvelleroy, Paris.

Exhibition Number: 21

20 Fan Leaf
Date: c. 1854

A woodblock colour print in the form of a fan, by Utagawa Kunisada (1786-1864), also known as Toyokuni III. In the foreground a courtesan picks her teeth while behind are scenes along the water's edge at Shinagawa.

29cm x 21cm

Provenance: Purchased in Japan by the owner's father who was an engineer in Japan during the 1920s. Ray Scott-White is a past Master of the Worshipful Company of Fan-Makers (1988-9). Lent by Ray Scott-White.

Exhibition Number: 23

21 Fan Leaf
Date: c. 1859

A woodblock colour print in the form of a fan, by Utagawa Kunisada (1786-1864), also known as Toyokuni III. In the foreground a courtesan, holding a pipe, is portrayed with the Kanda Myojin Shrine in the distance.

29cm x 22cm

Provenance: Lent by Ray Scott-White.

Exhibition Number: 24

22 Folding Fan
Date: Second half 19th century

A double paper leaf painted in ink and colours with the head and shoulders of a *bijin* ('beautiful woman'). The *reverse* is undecorated. Bamboo *sticks* and *guards*. The fan has a bamboo wedge *rivet*.

Total height	26.6cm
Width	43.2cm

Provenance: Formerly in the collection of Charlotte Salwey. Lent by John Salwey.

Exhibition Number: 25

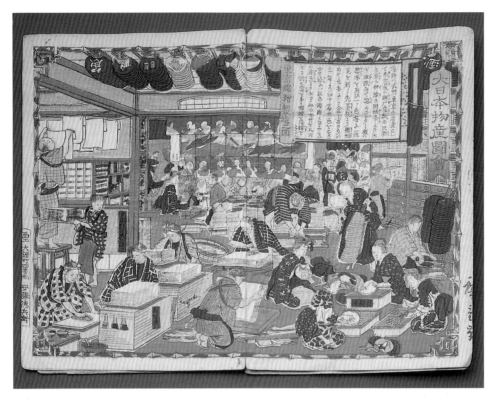

23 Woodblock Print
Date: 1880s

A double-page spread from a woodblock printed book entitled *Dai Nippon Bussau Zu-e* ('Drawings of the Products of Japan') by Tokubei Ando. This print illustrates the interior of a shop where the various stages of printing individual sheets from wooden blocks can be seen, together with the pasting of woodblock prints of the fan format on to frames of splayed bamboo splints. Finished *uchiwa* fans are stacked around the shop and hang from the ceiling.

24cm x17.5cm

Provenance: The Fan Museum, Hélène Alexander Collection.

Exhibition Number: 32

24 Folding Fan
Date: Last quarter 19th century

A double paper leaf painted on both sides in colour with birds and branches of maple leaves on a gold-flecked russet-coloured ground. Bamboo *sticks* and *guards*.

Total height	38cm
Width	74cm

Provenance: Formerly in the collection of Charlotte Salwey. Lent by John Salwey.

Exhibition Number: 38

25 Folding Fan
Date: Last quarter 19th century

A double paper leaf printed with part of the text
of a Noh theatre play, entitled *Takasuna*, and
inscribed *ko uta sen* ('small chant fan'). Bamboo
sticks and *guards*, the latter pierced with *nekome*
('cat's eyes') motifs. The fan has a bamboo
wedge and polished *rivet*.

Total height   27cm
Width   46cm

Provenance: The Fan Museum, Hélène Alexander Collection.

Exhibition Number: 39

26 Folding Fan
Date: c.1900

A double paper leaf with a seashore scene of the
fish industry on the island of Hokkaidō, printed
in black and colours on gold-sprinkled paper.
The *reverse* depicts a spray of prunus. Bamboo
sticks and *guards*. Inscribed "Hokkaidō *gyogyo
keikyo*" (The fish industry of Hokkaidō).

Total length   25.3cm
Width   46cm

Anonymous loan.

Exhibition Number: 40

Japanese Export Fans

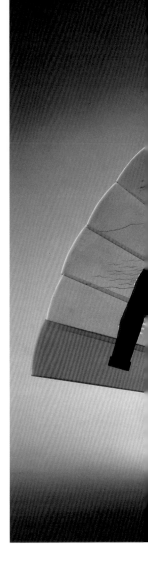

27 *Brisé* Fan

Date: Last quarter 19th century

Tortoiseshell *sticks* decorated in gold *hiramakie* and inlaid with mother-of-pearl. The scene of a peacock surrounded by flowers, bamboo, cranes and other birds is repeated on both faces of the fan. The *guards* are similarly decorated with gold lacquer inlaid with mother-of-pearl, depicting birds amongst floral sprays and branches. The fan is stored within a lacquer box with an inset glass lid of Chinese type. The fan has a metal *rivet* and *loop* with a silk *cord* and *tassel*.

Total length   30.5cm
Width   52cm

Anonymous loan.

Exhibition Number: 83

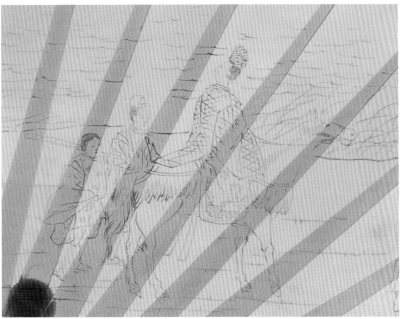

28 *Brisé* Fan

Date: Late 19th century

Blond tortoiseshell incised *sticks* with gold rubbed into the depressions. It depicts a courtier on horseback with his attendants making their way along the edge of a lake, with Mount Fuji in the far distance. The fan has a gold *rivet* and *loop*, with a black silk *cord* and *tassels*.

Total length 28cm
Width 52cm

Provenance: Lent by Michel Maignan, Duvelleroy, Paris.

Exhibition Number: 84

Reference: Illustrated in Maignan, Michel, '*Oji & uchiwa*', Bulletin association Franco-Japonaise, Paris, No. 18, October 1987, p.13, pl.34.

61

29 *Brisé* Fan

Date: Late 19th century

Tortoiseshell *sticks* decorated
with a man carrying a bundle of
firewood on his back, together
with thatched houses and trees
in the background, executed in
gold, silver and red *hiramakie*
with applied ivory for the face
and hands. The *reverse* depicts
two quails and butterflies
amongst flowers and grasses.
The *guards* are decorated with
birds amongst bamboo and trees
in gold and silver *hiramakie*,
enriched with *kirigane*.

Total height   25cm
Width   45cm

Provenance: Lent by Michel Maignan,
Duvelleroy, Paris.

Exhibition Number: 85

Reference: Illustrated in Maignan, Michel,
'*Ōji & uchiwa*', Bulletin association
Franco-Japonaise, Paris, No. 18,
October 1987, p.12, pl.33.

30 *Brisé* Fan

Date: Late 19th century

The fan is composed of ivory *sticks* and *guards* which are incised and stained black in places with a scene of three women, one of whom is playing the *koto*, a stringed musical instrument. They are surrounded by a landscape with Mount Fuji, irises, cranes and a *shishi* (lion-dog). The guards are decorated with flowering branches and two characters. The fact that the latter appear clumsily formed and are not readily recognisable suggests that they were produced by a craftsman who was not wholly familiar with the Chinese characters used in the Japanese written language. Although the design is overly 'Japanese' in a manner associated with Western rather than Japanese design, the details of the design are sufficiently accurate to suggest a close knowledge of Japanese iconography. Some exceptions are the symmetrical depiction of Mount Fuji and the somewhat uncharacteristic portrayal of the women's faces. It is uncertain, therefore, whether this fan was actually made in Japan or further afield. The fan has a cat's eye *rivet*.

Total height   23cm
Width   40cm

Provenance: The Fan Museum, Hélène Alexander Collection.

Exhibition Number: 22

31 *Brisé* Fan

Date: Late 19th century

Ivory *sticks* on which three of the Seven Sages of the Bamboo Grove and an attendant are depicted. They are executed in gold and silver *hiramakie* and *takamakie* with applied ivory faces and hands which are carved and stained black and red in places, together with inlaid mother-of-pearl. The *reverse* portrays a pair of quails with flowers and grasses by a stream. The *guards* are decorated with *hiramakie* and *takamakie* enriched with *kirigane*, together with encrustations of tortoiseshell, mother-of-pearl and other materials. The fan has a silver *loop* and filigree *rivet*, silk *cord* and *tassels* and an ivory *ojime* decorated with gold *hiramakie*.

Total length   30cm
Width   59cm

Provenance: The Fan Museum, Hélène Alexander Collection.

Exhibition Number: 87

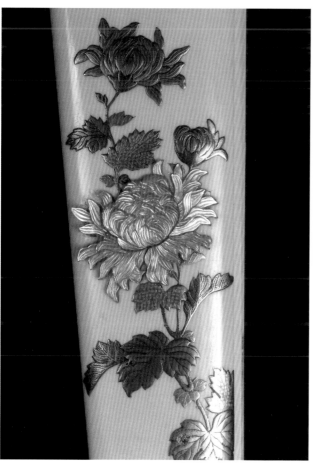

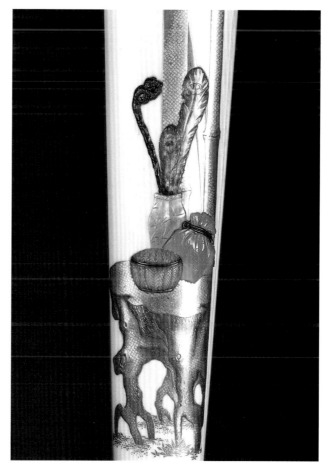

32 Brisé Fan
Date: Last quarter 19th century

Ivory *sticks* decorated with gold, silver and black *hiramakie*. One side portrays archaic vessels of Chinese origin such as the *ding* tripod, *jue* libation vessel and phoenix-headed ewer, as well as objects associated with the Chinese scholar's desk. The fan has an ivory and metal *rivet* and ivory *loop*, a silk *cord* and double silk *tassel*, with an ivory *ojime* decorated with gold *hiramakie*.

Total length	26cm
Width	46cm

Provenance: The Fan Museum, Hélène Alexander Collection.

Exhibition Number: 88

33 *Brisé* Fan

Date: Last quarter 19th century

Ivory *sticks* decorated with a peacock and peahen amongst flowers and a tree in gold and silver *hiramakie*. The *reverse* depicts a hilly landscape with trees and birds. The *guards* portray bamboo, flowers and insects in gold *hiramakie*, with encrustations in the Shibayama style. The fan has a metal *rivet* and *loop* with a silk *cord* and *tassels*. Ivory *ojime* in the form of a duck.

Total height   23.5cm
Width   41cm

Provenance: Lent by Michel Maignan, Duvelleroy, Paris.

Exhibition Number: 90

Reference: Illustrated in Maignan, Michel, '*Oji & uchiwa*', Bulletin association Franco-Japonaise, Paris, No. 18, October 1987, p.12, pl.32.

34 *Brisé* Fan

Date: Last quarter 19th century

Ivory *sticks* decorated with gold, silver, black and red *hiramakie* and *takamakie*, enriched with *kirigane*. The obverse portrays a courtier playing a flute among flowering plants, with hills in the background. The *reverse* depicts sheaves of straw drying on a pole, together with a hen, a maple branch and a fruiting tree. The *sticks* also reveal scalloped edges towards the rivet end. The *guards* are decorated with bamboo, flowers, grasses and birds in gold lacquer. The fan has a metal *rivet* and *loop*, silk *tassel* and an *ojime*.

Total length   20.3cm
Width   36cm

Anonymous loan.

Exhibition Number: 91

35 *Brisé* Fan

Date: Last quarter 19th century

Ivory *sticks* decorated with gold, silver and black *hiramakie* and *takamakie*, enriched with *kirigane*. The obverse portrays cranes amongst bamboo and flowers while the *reverse* depicts quails and flowers by a stream. The *guards* are decorated in the Shibayama style with birds, insects and flowers in minute encrustations of carved mother-of-pearl, tortoiseshell, hardstones and semi-precious stones. The fan has a metal *rivet* and metal *loop*, with silk *cord, tassels* and an ivory *ojime*.

Total length   26.5cm
Width   49cm

Anonymous loan.

Exhibition Number: 92

36 *Brisé* **Fan**

Date: Last quarter 19th century

Ivory *sticks* decorated with gold and black *hiramakie* and *takamakie*, enriched with *kirigane* and inlaid with carved ivory for the heads and feet of the figures. The obverse portrays a man and woman by a stream, crossed by a low bridge, a thatched hut and a lantern. The *reverse* depicts reeds growing in water with cranes flying above. The decoration of each *guard* complements the subject matter of the face of the fan with which it is seen. In addition, the fan is stored in a black lacquer box decorated with three folding fans in gold *hiramakie*. The fan has a silver *rivet* and *loop*, *cord* with *tassels* and an *ojime* decorated with gold *hiramakie*.

Total length	30cm
Width	52cm

Anonymous loan.

Exhibition Number: 93

37 *Brisé* Fan
Date: Last quarter 19th century

Bamboo *sticks* decorated with a drum, a *suehiro* ('wide-ended') folding fan, birds and flowers in gold, silver and black *hiramakie*. The *reverse* depicts a figure in a landscape. The *guards* are decorated with vines and birds in gold lacquer. The fan has a metal *rivet* and *loop*.

Total length   26.7cm
Width   49.5cm

Anonymous loan.

Exhibition Number: 94

38 *Brisé* Fan
Date: Last quarter 19th century

Bamboo *sticks* painted in colours with two figures in a hilly, wooded landscape. The *reverse* depicts a pair of pheasants under a pine tree and wisteria. One *guard* is painted with morning glory and the other with a figure under a tree, each complementing the subject matter of the face of the fan with which it is seen. Signed Kunihisa *ga* ('painted by Kunihisa'). The artist Kunihisa (1832-91) is recorded as being a pupil of the Ukiyoe print designer Kunisada. There are numerous fans for the export market with painted decoration signed by Kunihisa. The fan is accompanied by a plain wooden box with an encrusted figure of a woman. The fan has a metal *rivet* and *loop*, with a silk *cord* and *tassels*.

Total length   30cm
Width   56cm

Anonymous loan.

Exhibition Number: 116

References: For further examples see Maignan, Michel, 'Oji & uchiwa', Bulletin association Franco-Japonaise, Paris, Nos.26 and 27, October 1987, p.11 with signatures illustrated in nos. 29a and 29b. Also Iröns, John Neville, *Fans of Imperial Japan*, Hong Kong, 1981, p.21, pl.30 and pl.31.

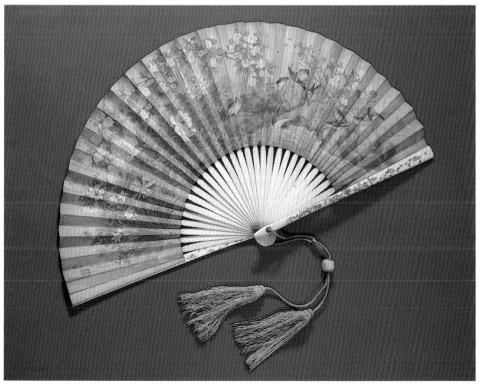

39 Folding Fan
Date: Last quarter 19th century

A double paper leaf covered with silk gauze and painted in colour. One side depicts three peasants with bundles of straw in a hilly, wooded landscape. The *reverse* portrays birds and flowers by the edge of a stream. Signed Nankoku Ozawa *saku* ('made by Nankoku Ozawa') with seal. Ivory *sticks* with scalloped edges. Ivory *guards* decorated with flowers and insects in gold *hiramakie* and encrustations in the Shibayama style.

Total height 28cm
Width 51cm

Anonymous loan.

Exhibition Number: 97

40 Folding Fan

Date: Late 19th century

A double paper fan leaf covered with silk and painted with a newly married couple receiving guests, with a priest seated behind them. The *reverse* depicts cranes in a landscape. Ivory *sticks* with scalloped edges. Ivory *guards* with insects and flowers encrusted in the Shibayama style. The fan has a metal *rivet* and an elaborate mauve and white *tassel* with a silk *cord* and an *ojime* with a gold lacquer ladybird.

Total height	27cm
Width	48cm

Provenance: The Fan Museum, Hélène Alexander Collection.

Exhibition Number: 100

41 Folding Fan

Date: Last quarter 19th century

A double leaf covered with silk gauze and painted with five figures in the foreground, together with an inset of a village with decorations for a festival. The *reverse* portrays a bird flying above flowers and shrubs. Bamboo *sticks* with scalloped edges and ivory *guards* encrusted with insects in the Shibayama style. The fan has a metal *rivet*.

Total length	27cm
Width	52cm

Provenance: Formerly in the collection of Charlotte Salwey. Lent by John Salwey.

Exhibition Number: 98

Reference: Illustrated in Salwey, Charlotte M., *Fans of Japan*, London, 1894, pl.111.

42 Folding Fan

Date: Dated the second year of Meiji, that is, 1869

A double paper leaf covered with silk gauze and painted in bright colours on a gold-flecked ground. One side depicts 13 figures dressed in their finery while, on the *reverse*, are two birds under a tree and by a stream. Signed Unro Tamehisa with seals. Bamboo *sticks* with scalloped edges. Ivory *guards* encrusted with insects in the Shibayama style. The fan has a metal *rivet*, with *cord, tassel* and a faceted *ojime*, which is lacquered.

Total length	26.5cm
Width	50cm

Anonymous loan.

Exhibition Number: 109

43 Folding Fan

Date: Last quarter 19th century

A double paper leaf painted in colour with a mature tree, thatched cottage and cranes in a misty landscape. The *reverse* is painted with a cock, hen, chick and dragonflies beneath a flowering shrub. Ivory *sticks* with scalloped edges. Ivory *guards* decorated with a trailing gourd and insects in gold *hiramakie* and encrustations in the Shibayama style.

Total height	27cm
Width	44cm

Provenance: The Fan Museum, Hélène Alexander Collection.

Exhibition Number: 101

44 Folding Fan

Date: Last quarter 19th century

A double paper leaf painted with flowers growing by a stream and birds flying above. The *reverse* depicts a rural scene in a snowstorm. Bamboo *sticks* with scalloped edges and ivory *guards* with two encrusted insects on one guard and only one insect on the other. The fan has a metal *rivet* and *loop* with a *cord* and silk *tassel,* and an ivory *ojime* with encrusted insects to complement those on the guards.

Total height   27cm
Width   40cm

Provenance: The Fan Museum, Hélène Alexander Collection.

Exhibition Number: 103

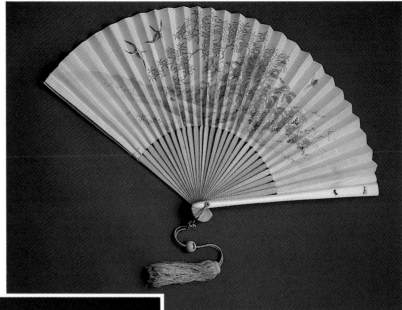

45 Folding Fan

Date: Last quarter 19th century

A double paper leaf painted in ink and colour with women washing lengths of silk and drying them on the banks of a river. The *reverse* with three cartouches depicting a crane, a man smoking and two swallows and wisteria respectively against a gold background. Bamboo *sticks* with scalloped edges and ivory *guards* with insects encrusted in the Shibayama style. The fan is stored in its own case of woven bamboo. The fan has a metal *rivet.*

Total length   27cm
Width   55cm

Provenance: The Fan Museum, Hélène Alexander Collection.

Exhibition Number: 104

46 Folding Fan

Date: Last quarter 19th century

A double paper leaf painted with cranes amongst flowers on a gold ground. The *reverse* portrays a variety of different fishes painted in colours. Ivory *sticks* and *guards*, the latter with encrustations of birds and insects under wisteria blooms in the Shibayama style. The top part of the guards can be made to slide over the bottom part, thus reducing the overall size of the fan. When this is done the leaves, which are attached to the upper part of the guards, also slide over the sticks. It is for this reason that this type of fan is termed 'telescopic'. The fan has a metal *rivet* and *loop*, with a mauve silk *tassel* on a *cord*, together with an *ojime* encrusted in the Shibayama style.

Total length   (a) extended 18cm
                             (b) closed 14cm
Width   33cm

Exhibition Number: 105

Reference: Volet, Maryse, *L'invention au service de l'Eventail*, Geneva, 1986, p.23, Patent No. 197.

47 Folding Fan

Date: Last quarter 19th century

A double paper leaf covered with silk gauze and painted in colours on a gold-sprinkled ground. One side depicts a pair of pheasants amongst peonies with butterflies flying above, while the *reverse* portrays a misty landscape. Ivory *sticks* decorated with three cranes in gold and silver *hiramakie*. Ivory *guards* with vines, flowers, birds and insects in lacquer, enriched with *kirigane* and Shibayama-style encrustations. The fan has a silver *loop* and *rivet*, silk *cord* and *tassel*, and an *ojime* decorated with gold lacquer.

Total length   29cm
Width   53.3cm

Anonymous loan.

Exhibition Number: 108

48 Folding Fan

Date: Last quarter 19th century

A double paper leaf with a man on a boat in a river landscape painted in colours on a gold-flecked ground. The *reverse* depicts irises and peonies growing on the banks of a stream in which fish are swimming. Ivory *sticks* and *guards*, the latter with flowering plants and insects in gold *hiramakie* and encrustations in the Shibayama style. The fan has a metal *loop* and *rivet*, silk *tassels* and *cord*, and an *ojime* decorated in gold *hiramakie*.

Total length	30cm
Width	53cm

Anonymous loan.

Exhibition Number: 110

49 Folding Fan

Date: Last quarter 19th century

A double paper leaf painted in colour with roundels on one side, which portray men and women promenading or engaged in leisure activities, on a gold ground. Ivory *sticks* with scalloped edges. Ivory *guards* carved and decorated in gold and silver *hiramakie*, with bamboo and morning glory on one guard and a woman with flowering prunus on the other. The fan has a metal *loop* and *rivet*, silk *cord* and *tassel*, and a lacquered *ojime*.

Total height	26.6cm
Width	47cm

Anonymous loan.

Exhibition Number: 111

50 Folding Fan
Date: Last quarter 19th century

A double paper leaf covered with silk gauze and painted with lotus flowers, leaves and a crane in flight in green, pink, white and black. Signed Doitsu with seal. The *reverse* portrays quails amongst flowers and grasses in ink only. An inscription reads "I live in Tokyo but retreat to Taikyo Kayama". Ivory *sticks* and *guards*, the latter with bamboo and plants in gold *hiramakie* with encrustations in the Shibayama style. The fan has a metal *rivet* and *loop* with silk *cord* and *tassels* and an ivory *ojime* decorated with gold *hiramakie*.

| Total height | 33cm |
| Width | 58.5cm |

Anonymous loan.

Exhibition Number: 112

51 Folding Fan

Date: Last quarter 19th century

A double paper asymmetric leaf covered with silk gauze and painted with figures in a snowy landscape. The *reverse* portrays birds and flowers by a stream. Ivory *sticks* and *guards*, the latter decorated with cranes and insects amongst bamboo and flowers in gold *hiramakie* and Shibayama-style encrustations. The asymmetric folding fan was a type introduced from the West which was manufactured in Japan for the export market. The fan has a metal *loop* and silk *tassel*.

Total length   69cm
Width   52cm

Anonymous loan.

Exhibition Number: 113

52 Folding Fan

Date: Late 19th century

A double paper leaf painted with a figure by a lake, set against mountains in the background. The *reverse* depicts a butterfly and flowers. Bamboo *sticks* with scalloped edges. The ivory *guards*, which are incised and encrusted with mother-of-pearl, tortoiseshell and semi-precious stones, depict a flowering branch and ladybirds. At the top of each guard is an inlaid metal figure of a man and a woman respectively. The fan has a metal *rivet* and *cord*, together with *tassels*.

Total height   27cm
Width   49.5cm

Anonymous loan.

Exhibition Number: 114

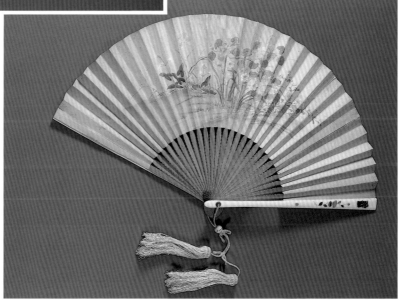

53 Shibayama Samples
Date: Late 19th century

Three sheets of paper, each with ten small carvings of birds in mother-of-pearl, ivory, tortoiseshell and semi-precious stones. Each bird is set against a background of flowers, grasses or tree branches painted in ink and colours. Such carvings were originally designed to be inlaid or encrusted into a lacquer or ivory base to form elements of the design. This type of decoration was commonly associated with the Shibayama family, though there were many other craftsmen who worked in a similar style. (For further details see p.31.)

Anonymous loan.

Exhibition Number: 107

54 Folding Fan
Date: 1880s

A double paper leaf painted with birds flying over a stream, along the banks of which grow irises, lilies and peonies on a gold-flecked ground. The *reverse* depicts butterflies flying over a clump of similar flowers. Bamboo *sticks* and *guards*, the latter decorated with branches of blossom in gold and red *hiramakie*. The characters, which are partly visible on one of the guards where the paper leaf has lifted, read '28', and refer to the number of *sticks* used in the mounting of this fan. The fan has a metal *rivet* with *cord* and *tassels*. The cuboid *ojime* is decorated with an encrusted fly.

Total length   30.5cm
Width   51cm

Anonymous loan.

Exhibition Number: 115

55 Folding Fan
Date: Early 20th century

A double silk gauze leaf painted in ink and colours with three geese by the edge of a lake surrounded by reeds, with a full moon behind. The ivory *sticks* are incised and partly cut through to the other side. The ivory *guards* are deeply carved with a bird on a flowering branch. The painted design on the silk gauze is clearly visible on the *reverse*, while the ivory *sticks* which support the leaves can be seen on either side. The fan has a metal *rivet* and *loop*.

Total height   24cm
Width   45.5cm

Anonymous loan.

Exhibition Number: 117

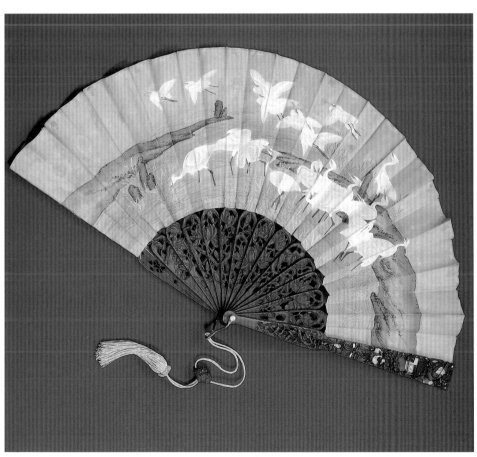

56 Folding Fan
Date: c. 1900

A single silk leaf painted in ink and colour, with cranes standing in the water at the edge of a lake or in flight above. Open-work wooden *sticks* carved with flowers. The *guards* are similarly carved with a figure playing a flute, birds, a thatched hut, trees and flowers, and inlaid with mother-of-pearl, horn and ivory.

Total length   30.5cm
Width   56cm

Anonymous loan.

Exhibition Number: 119

57 Folding Fan
Date: Late 19th century

A double paper leaf painted with a rural scene of harvesting. The *reverse* depicts peasants in a winter landscape. Tortoiseshell *sticks* and *guards*, the latter decorated with wisteria and butterflies in gold *hiramakie* and encrustations. The fan has a metal *rivet* and *loop*, silk *tassel* and *cord*, together with an ivory *ojime* decorated with gold lacquer.

Total length 28cm
Width 53.5cm

Anonymous loan.

Exhibition Number: 122

58a Folding Fan
Date: c. 1885-7

A double paper leaf painted in colours with a bird flying amongst chrysanthemums and stylized clouds flecked with silver squares. The plain paper on the *reverse* is signed by members of the cast of *The Mikado*, a light opera by Gilbert and Sullivan. Bamboo *sticks* and *guards*. The fan has a metal *rivet* and small metal ring.

Total height	33cm
Width	62cm

Provenance: Together with the signatures, the reverse of the fan is inscribed "This is the fan of Willie Elliots (Koko)". Willie Elliots was the first Koko in *The Mikado*, the first production of which took place between 14th March 1885 and 19th January 1887. Although one cannot be certain that this fan was actually used by Koko in the first production, the fact that the other signatures are those of the early cast and that the size of the fan is in keeping with fashion of the late 1880s would suggest that it was used in one of the early performances. The Fan Museum, Hélène Alexander Collection.

Exhibition Number: 123

58b Folding Fan
Date: c. 1885-90

Double paper leaf painted in colour with birds flying over flowers and grasses growing by a stream. The plain paper on the *reverse* is signed by members of the cast of *The Mikado*. Bamboo *sticks* and *guards*. The fan has a metal *rivet* and *loop*.

Total height	36cm
Width	63.5cm

Provenance: Some of the signatures on this fan differ from those found on No. 58A while others refer to the same members of cast. The photographs, which were purchased with the fan, are of members of the D'Oyly Carte Opera Company, one of which is dated 1888.

Lent by The Fan Museum, Hélène Alexander Collection.

Exhibition Numbers: 124

59 Folding Fan

Date: Late 19th–early 20th century

A double paper leaf painted on both sides with birds amongst flowers and grasses in white, grey and pale yellow on a black ground. Stained wooden *sticks* and *guards*. The fan has a metal *rivet* with two small circular links attached on either side.

Total height   33.7cm
Width   58.5cm

Provenance: The Fan Museum, Hélène Alexander Collection.

Exhibition Number: 126

60 Folding Fan

Date: Late 19th century

A double paper leaf covered with silk gauze and embroidered in silk and gold threads, with painted details. On one side, a bird is depicted on a flowering plant with embroidered flowers and painted leaves. The *reverse* portrays three butterflies amongst flowers. Bamboo *sticks* and *guards*, the latter decorated with birds, flowers and insects in gold lacquer and Shibayama-style encrustations.

Total height   30cm
Width   54cm

Anonymous loan.

Exhibition Number: 127

61 Folding Fan
Date: Late 19th century

A double paper leaf with birds settling on the branches of a tree in blossom, painted in colour on a gold-flecked ground. The *reverse* depicts ducks swimming in a lake surrounded by reeds, or flying above. Black lacquered *sticks* with birds amongst flowers in gold *hiramakie*. Black lacquered *guards* with butterflies in gold *hiramakie* and *takamakie*. The fan has a metal *rivet* with a silk cord *tassel*.

Total height   30cm
Width   55cm

Provenance: The Fan Museum, Hélène Alexander Collection.

Exhibition Number: 128

62 Folding Fan

Date: 1920s

A double paper leaf painted in ink and colours with irises on one side, and figures of women and men on the other. The *guards* are decorated with gold *hiramakie* on a black lacquer ground. The mechanism of this cockade fan works by pulling a cord at the top, whereupon the fan retracts into the guards, which form a box-like contraption when the tassel is pulled at the bottom.

Total length	28cm
Diameter of fully open leaf	30cm

Provenance: The Fan Museum, Hélène Alexander Collection.

Exhibition Number: 130

Reference: Volet, Maryse, *L'invention au service de l'eventail*, Geneva, 1986, p.84, Patent No.109.

Advertising, Commemorative and Contemporary Fans

63 Folding Fan
Date: c. 1876

A double paper leaf printed in black on white against a blue border. The fan depicts part of a circle around the edge of which are the words "Proclaim Liberty throughout all the land unto all the inhabitants thereof". It contains a bell inscribed 1776, under which is a river and suspension bridge, steamships, a steam engine, a hot-air balloon inscribed 1876, a soldier and a cannon. To the left is a stylised monogram and to the right, two cranes flying towards the circle. The *reverse* is printed with a bird and a spray of blossom. Black lacquered wooden *sticks* and *guards*. This fan was one of the many Japanese fans produced to commemorate the Centennial Exhibition in Philadelphia, 1876, which celebrated 100 years of American Independence.

Total height   28cm
Width   50cm

Provenance: Lent by Michel Maignan, Duvelleroy, Paris.

Exhibition Number: 133

64 Folding Fan
Date: c. 1910

A single silver-flecked paper leaf printed with three photographic portraits of Prince Fushimi (centre), Admiral Yamamoto (left) and General Nishi (right). The portraits are surrounded by irises painted in colour. This fan was produced to commemorate the Anglo-Japanese Exhibition of 1910 held at the White City in Shepherd's Bush, London. The *reverse* shows the plain flecked paper with the *sticks* visible where they are stuck to the leaf. The shaped wooden sticks and *guards* are painted with flowers. The fan has a metal *rivet* and *loop*.

Total height   23cm
Width   41cm

Provenance: The Fan Museum, Hélène Alexander Collection.

Exhibition Number: 134

Reference: The Fan Circle International, *Royal Fans*, Catalogue No. 126, 1986, p.54.

65 Folding Fan
Date: c. 1912

A double paper leaf printed with the Japanese flag and the White Ensign (Royal Navy) which are crossed and joined by a cord and tassels. The fan is inscribed "Souvenir of Visit to Yenoshima and Kamakura 1912". The *reverse* is undecorated silver-flecked paper. Bamboo *sticks* and *guards*. The fan has a wedge bamboo *rivet*.

Friendly relations between the two countries had been cemented with the Anglo-Japanese Exhibition of 1910. It was customary to produce such fans as a souvenir of major exhibitions.

Total length 26.6cm
Width 45cm

Provenance: The Fan Museum, gift of Mrs Rosabella Gardner.

Exhibition Number: 135

66 Folding Fan
Date: c. 1912-13

A double paper leaf printed on one side with a calendar for the year 1913. The illustrations allude to various festivals, activities and seasonal flowers during the months of the year, such as the Girl's Festival in March and the Boy's Festival in May. The *reverse* is plain silver-flecked paper. Black lacquered wooden *sticks* and *guards*. The fan has a metal *rivet* and *loop*.

Total height 23cm
Width 45cm

Provenance: The Fan Museum, Hélène Alexander Collection.

Exhibition Number: 136

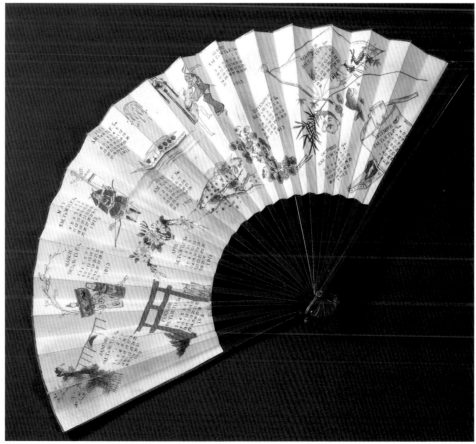

67 Folding Fan
Date: Early 20th century

A double paper leaf printed with famous beauty spots around Japan, such as Izu hot springs and Amano Hashidate, renowned for its pine trees, all contained within shaped cartouches. Bamboo *sticks* and *guards*. The fan has a metal *rivet*.

Total height	25cm
Width	44cm

Provenance: The Fan Museum, Hélène Alexander Collection.

Exhibition Number: 138

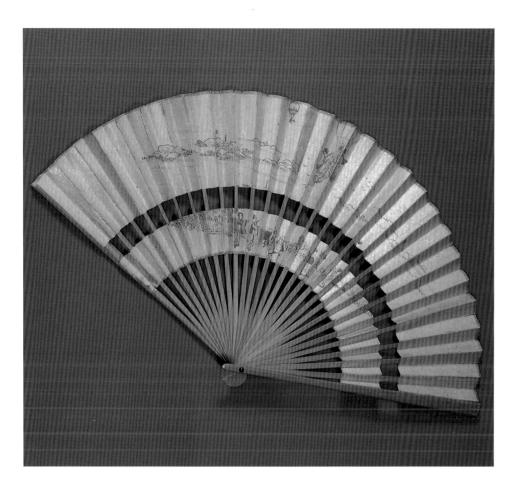

68 Folding Fan
Date: Late 19th-early 20th century

A *cabriolet* fan with each concentric ring made of a double paper leaf. It is printed on one side only with women and children watching hot-air ballooning. Bamboo *sticks* and *guards*. The fan has a metal *rivet*.

Total height	19.5cm
Width	37cm

Anonymous loan.

Exhibition Number: 137

69 Folding Fan
Date: Late 19th-early 20th century

A double paper leaf painted with Mount Fuji in black, grey and white. Signed Hanko with seals. The fan is also inscribed with a poem about Mount Fuji. Along the paper leaf by the guard is stamped "Restaurant Drouant Rue Gaillon Paris". On the *reverse* is printed "Restaurant Drouant – Rue Gaillon – Paris" and *"Importé du Japon"*. Bamboo *sticks* and *guards*. The fan has a metal *rivet*.

From the late 19th century to the 1930s, Japanese fans were imported in vast quantities to Europe and America and were often used for advertising purposes, especially by restaurants. The name of the establishment was usually stamped on the leaf or along the guards of the fan.

Total length	27.3cm
Width	47.5cm

Provenance: Lent by Michel Maignan, Duvelleroy, Paris.

Exhibition Number: 140

91

70 Folding Fan
Date: 1920s–30s

A double paper leaf printed with Mount Fuji, a lake and trees. Signed Shunkyo with seal. The *reverse* advertises the shop of J. N. Ramsamy & Bros. in Colombo, Ceylon, as the place to buy souvenirs. Bamboo *sticks* and *guards*.

Total height	24cm
Width	39.5cm

Provenance: The Fan Museum, Hélène Alexander Collection.

Exhibition Number: 141

71 Folding Fan
Date: c. 1980s

A double paper leaf printed with cranes flying over the sea against a pink sky. The *reverse* indicates that this fan was given to passengers of Japan Airlines to commemorate crossing the North Pole. Spaces have been left for the individual to fill in the date, flight number and his or her name. Black lacquered wooden *sticks* and *guards*. The fan has a plastic *rivet*.

Total height	27.2cm
Width	48cm

Provenance: The Fan Museum.

Exhibition Number: 144

72 Folding Fan

Date: Contemporary

A double paper leaf printed on both sides with useful words, phrases and expressions in English and Japanese to help the tourist in Japan. Such phrases include "Speak more slowly please", "Where is the fire exit?" and ''I want a double room''. Each expression is also printed in romanized Japanese to help the foreigner pronounce it. Bamboo *sticks* and *guards*. The fan has a plastic *rivet* with a nylon *cord* to which a miniature magnifying glass is attached.

Total height   22.1cm
Width   35.5cm

Provenance: The Fan Museum, gift of Mrs Rosabella Gardner.

Exhibition Number: 146

73 Folding Fan

Date: 1950s–early 60s

A double paper leaf printed on one side with a car parked amongst trees with two people enjoying a picnic. To the left is the logo of the Nissan Corporation. Bamboo *sticks* and *guards*. The fan has a plastic *rivet*.

Span of leaf   36cm

Anonymous loan.

Exhibition Number: 147b

74 Folding Fan
Date: 1960s

A double paper leaf with a painted Noh mask applied to dark red ground. Gold seal (unread). The *reverse* is plain gold-flecked paper. Black lacquered wooden *sticks* and *guards*. The fan has a metal *rivet*.

Total height   36.5cm
Width   51cm

Provenance: Formerly in the collection of Bertha de Vere Green. The Fan Museum, Hélène Alexander Collection.

Exhibition Number: 57

75 Folding Fan
Date: Contemporary

A double paper leaf painted with two bands of stylized water on both sides in purple and gold against a gold ground. Bamboo *sticks* and *guards*, the latter with pierced designs resembling the *nekome* ('cat's eyes') motif. The fan has a bamboo *rivet*.

Total height   33cm
Width   56cm

Provenance: This fan is from the Kanze school of Noh drama and was acquired in Japan in 1989. All Noh drama fans are made today by distantly related members of one family working in several workshops in Kyoto.

Anonymous loan.

Exhibition Number: 59

76 Folding Fan

Date: Contemporary

A double paper leaf painted on both sides with pink, blue and yellow clematis on stylized water represented by blue whorls on a gold ground. The *reverse* depicts an almost identical design on a silver ground. Black lacquered wooden *sticks* and *guards*, the latter with pierced designs resembling the *nekome* ('cat's eyes') motif.

Total height	32.5cm
Width	55cm

Provenance: This is a limited edition Noh fan of the Kanze school, which is one of five Noh schools in Kyoto. It was made to commemorate the death of a famous drummer. Water is a symbol that appears on all the fans used by members of the Kanze school whether they be actors, singers or drummers. The design on the guards is also unique to the Kanze school.

Anonymous loan.

Exhibition Number: 60

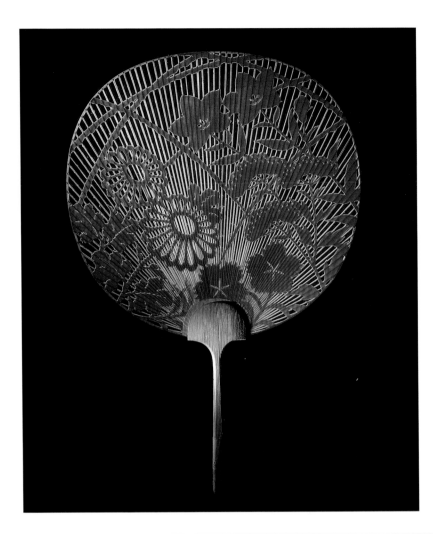

77 Fixed Fan
Date: Contemporary

A fixed fan made of bamboo split into numerous thin splints which are secured around the edges. Cut red paper flowers are applied to the splints. Bamboo handle.

Leaf	25.5cm x 25cm
Length of handle	17cm

Provenance: Made by Mr Aiba of Kyoto. Mr Aiba is the ninth generation of *uchiwa* makers. His family supplied the imperial court and he has written several books on the subject of *uchiwa*. He is a member of the Fanmakers' Guild of Kyoto.

Anonymous loan.

Exhibition Number: 61

78 Folding Fan
Date: c. 1990

A single silk gauze leaf with applied cut red paper flowers and grasses with touches of silver. Shaped bamboo *sticks* and plain *guards*, one of which is signed Junkichi N. The fan has a metal *rivet* and *loop*.

Total height	21.5cm
Width	38cm

Provenance: This fan was given to the owner by Mrs Eiko Nakanishi whose family have made this type of 'cut out' summer fan for generations.

Anonymous loan.

Exhibition Number: 62

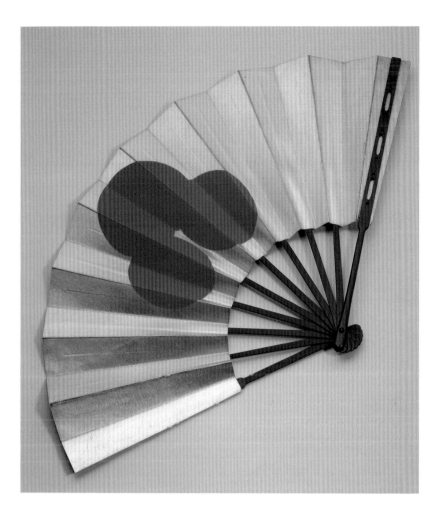

79 Folding Fan
Date: Contemporary

A double paper leaf painted with red circles on a gold ground. The *reverse* reveals a similar design on a silver ground. Black lacquered wooden *sticks* and *guards*, the latter with pierced designs.

Total height   32.5cm
Width   55cm

Provenance: A Gion Festival fan. The Gion Festival, a merchant's festival and one of the biggest in Japan, takes place in Kyoto on 17th July. The fans are carried by two men who stand at the front of each decorated *yamaboko* float. There are 33 different kinds of Gion Festival fan, all made by the Ohshima family.

Anonymous loan.

Exhibition Number: 65

80 Folding Fan
Date: 20th century

A double paper leaf printed with a scene of a ceremonial occasion at the Gosho Royal Palace, Kyoto. The *reverse* with undecorated silver-flecked paper. Bamboo *sticks* and *guards*. The fan has a bamboo wedge *rivet*.

Total height   26.5cm
Width   45cm

Anonymous loan.

Exhibition Number: 78

81 Folding Fan
Date: Contemporary

A double paper leaf painted with flowers in a cart amongst stylized clouds of gold and red. Black lacquered wooden *sticks* and *guard*. The *reverse* reveals undecorated gold-flecked paper. The fan has a plastic *rivet*.

Total height 22.2cm
Width 39.3cm

Anonymous loan.

Exhibition Number: 79

Fan related objects

82 Fan Game
Date: Contemporary

A wooden box which is decorated with raised white flowers and painted green leaves. On the box stands a weighted target in the form of a *gingko* leaf covered in silk, from which hang two bells. Behind the box is a folding fan made up of a double pink paper leaf with bamboo *sticks* and *guards*.

Total height	17.5cm
Sides	9cm

Provenance: Tōsenkyo ('the pleasure of throwing a fan') became popular during the late 18th century; the game is played with a folding fan which is thrown at a target in the form of a *gingko* leaf. The target is placed on a box which is about six inches tall. As it can be played indoors, it became especially popular with women and children. When men joined in and started gambling on the results, the game was subject to prohibitions. As an innocent game it continued to be played until the Meiji period. This particular *tōsenkyo* was given to the owner by Mr Shinbee Miyawaki in 1989.

Anonymous loan.

Exhibition Number: 82

83 Kakiemon Dishes
Date: Early 18th century

A set of five Kakiemon dishes in the shape of fans painted with a prunus branch emerging from rockwork in underglaze blue, turquoise, yellow and iron red. The lower part is delicately engraved with scrolling patterns and coloured in underglaze blue. The *reverse* with tasselled cash above a comb foot.

Width	16.8cm

Provenance: Lent by Spink & Son Ltd, London.

Exhibition Number: 132B

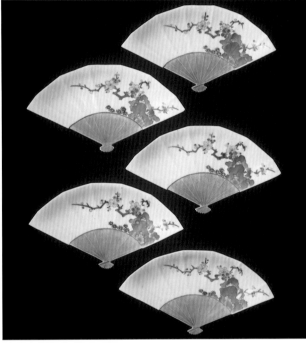

84 Satsuma Vase
Date: 19th century

An important Satsuma-ware vase of baluster form. The sides decorated with two exquisitely detailed fan-shaped panels, one containing a scene of ducks on a lake, and the other a study of a group of fish. Each panel is signed Sozan, one panel signed Kyoto Kinkozan Zo, Sozan.

Total height	22cm

Provenance: Lent by Spink & Son Ltd, London.

Exhibition Number: 84

85 A Shop Sign for a Fan Shop
Date: Late Edo period (1615–1868)

A wooden shop sign in the shape of a folding fan painted, on one side only, with three Chinese sages amongst clouds. The *sticks* and *guards* are painted black.

Total height	64.5cm
Width	102cm

Provenance: The Fan Museum, gift from the Victor Adda Foundation.

Exhibition Number: 2

Reference: Barbara Ford of the Metropolitan Museum of Art, New York, has remarked that it is one of the finest shop signs of its kind and period.

86 A Pair of Hair Ornaments
Date: Early 20th century

Two tiny fans, one a folding fan and the other a *brisé* fan, mounted on to lacquered wooden pins for wearing in the traditional elaborate hairstyle of a Japanese woman. Both fans are painted with flowers.

1 Total length	14cm
Span of fan	7.2cm
2 Total length	16.5cm
Span of fan	6cm

Provenance: Lent by Michel Maignan, Duvelleroy, Paris.

Exhibition Number: 29

87 Lacquer Box
Date: Late 19th century

A box and cover in the form of a folding fan leaf with irises in gold *hiramakie* on a black lacquer ground.

9cm x 4cm

Provenance: Lent by Michel Maignan, Duvelleroy, Paris.

Exhibition Number: 35

88 Black Lacquer Box
Date: Late 19th century

A box and cover in the form of a folding fan decorated with buildings in a landscape in gold *hiramakie* on a black lacquer ground.

9cm x 6cm

Provenance: The Fan Museum, Hélène Alexander Collection.

Exhibition Number: 121

89 Ivory Box
Date: 19th century

An ivory cosmetic box and cover in the form of a folding fan, decorated with cranes flying over waves with the sun in the background, painted in gold, green and red.

5.5cm x 3.7cm

Provenance: Lent by Michel Maignan, Duvelleroy, Paris.

Exhibition Number: 33

90 Ivory Box
Date: 19th century

A square ivory cosmetic box and cover deeply carved with a book and an *uchiwa* on a background of flowers. The details painted in gold, red and green.

5cm x 5cm

Provenance: Lent by Michel Maignan, Duvelleroy, Paris.

Exhibition Number: 34

91 Black lacquer box
Date: Second half 19th century

A box with a swivel cover shaped in the form of a closed folding fan. Black lacquered wood with pheonixes and flowers inlaid with mother-of-pearl, tortoiseshell and stained ivory. The *rivet* of the fan, which conceals the swivel pin, is in the form of metal maple leaves. The interior of the box is lined with silk. The underside of the box reveals the original label indicating that it was sold through Liberty's store for the sum of 35/-. (For more details of Liberty's department store see p.29.)

Length   34cm

Provenance: Lent by Michel Maignan, Duvelleroy, Paris.

Photography by Jean Lambert.

Exhibition Number: 120

92 *Inrō*
Date: Late Edo period

A fine and unusual sheath *inrō*, the outer case decorated in *takamakie* and *hiramakie* with peony, chrysanthemums, reeds and irises on a bright gold ground, all bordered with brilliant green-blue abalone shell mosaic inlaid in gold, silver and coloured shell roundels; the interior decorated in *togidashi* with interlocking fans, the ends matching the borders of the outer case.

Height   8.3cm

Provenance: Lent by Spink & Son Ltd, London.

93 A Miniature Book
Date: 1905

The Book of the Fan with rhymes by Walter Copeland and drawings by Charles Robinson, published by Blackie and Son Ltd in 1905. A miniature book with many illustrations of people on fans with verses about them, which emphasize the influence of the Japanese craze and the Japanese fan even into children's books. The cover of the book depicts a Japanese lady holding a folding fan with a crane in flight.

7cm x 9cm

Anonymous loan.

Exhibition Number: 131

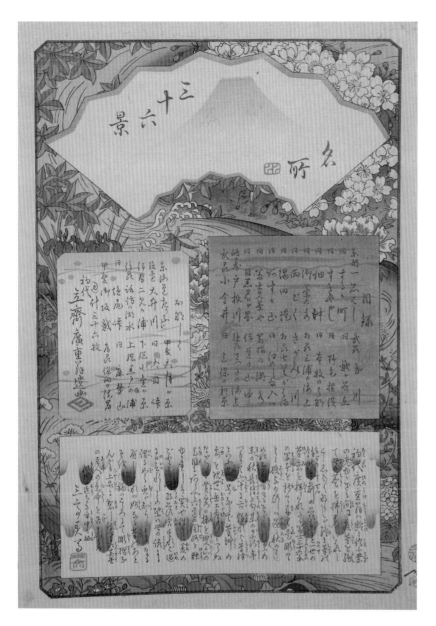

94 Contents page for a set of prints
Date: Dated 1859

The page of contents from a set of woodblock prints entitled *Thirty Six Views of Mount Fuji* by Andō Hiroshige (1797-1858). The title is contained within the outline of a folding fan leaf, together with Mount Fuji.

Provenance: This set of woodblock prints was published in 1859, the year after Hiroshige's death, by the publisher Tsutaya Kichizo who mentions his collaboration with Hiroshige in the preface. Lent by Ray Scott-White.

Exhibition Number: 41

95 Cast Iron Trivet
Date: Late 19th century

A cast iron trivet in the form of a folding fan set with three feet on the underside. The fan is decorated with a tortoise and a crane, both symbols of longevity.

Span of the top	23.5cm
Length of side	19cm

Provenance: The Fan Museum, Hélène Alexander Collection.

Exhibition Number: 42

96 Length of cloth
Date: Late 19th-early 20th century

Gold and blue silk cloth woven with repeating motifs of folding fans in alternate rows decorated with large or small drums and a flute. Hanging from the guards of the fans with the large drums are miniature helmets.

Length	210cm
Width	70cm

Anonymous loan.

Exhibition Number: 132

97 Portable Cabinet
Date: Second half 19th century

A portable cabinet on a low stand with inner drawers decorated in gold, silver and red *hiramakie* on a gold-sprinkled black lacquer ground. The cabinet depicts open and closed folding fans on stylized water. This alludes to a pastime in court circles of casting fans into a stream and composing a poem in the time it took before the fan sank.

Total height	19cm
Length	17cm
Width	12cm

Provenance: Lent by Michel Maignan, Duvelleroy, Paris.

Photography by Jean Lambert.

Exhibition Number: 51

Bibliography

Adburgham, Alison, 'Taking Liberty's: the story of a London store and Japan', *Japan digest*, Vol. 2, No. 1, July 1991.

Akiyama, Terukazu, *Japanese painting*, Cleveland, Ohio, 1961.

Chiba, Reiko, *Painted fans of Japan: fifteen Noh-drama masterpieces*, Rutland, Vermont and Tokyo, 1962.

Dawes, Leonard G., 'The nicely calculated flutter of the fan', *The Antique dealer and collectors guide*, London, March 1974, pp. 73-77.

Debrett's Peerage in association with The Fan Circle and the Victoria and Albert Museum, *Fans from the East*, London, 1978.

Earle, Joe, 'Fans and fan painting in Japan', *Connoisseur*, London, March 1979, pp. 191-194.

Earle, Joe, *Japanese prints*, London, 1980.

Gitter, Kurt A., *Japanese fan paintings*, New Orleans, 1985.

Hart, Ernest, 'The fans of the Far East', *The Queen*, 28th January 1893, pp. 136-137.

Hempel, Rose, *The Heian civilization of Japan*, Oxford, 1983.

Hillier, Jack Ronald, *The Harari collection of Japanese paintings and drawings*, III, Kanō, Decorative (Rimpa school), Nanga and Maruyama/Shijō schools, independents, fans of various schools, London, 1973.

Hillier, Jack Ronald, *The Japanese print: a new approach*, London, 1960.

Hosley, William, *The Japan idea*, Hartford, Connecticut, 1990.

Hutt, Julia, *Understanding Far Eastern art*, Oxford, 1987.

Ienaga, Saburo, *Painting in the Yamato style*, New York and Tokyo, 1973.

Iröns, Neville John, *Fans of Imperial Japan*, Hong Kong, 1981.

Iröns, Neville John, 'Japanese fans of the Meiji period', *Arts of Asia*, March-April 1983, pp. 62-71.

Joly, Henri L., *Legend in Japanese art*, London, 1908.

Kyoto National Museum, *Senmen koshakyō* ('Decorated sutra fan leaves'), Kyoto, 1930.

Lane, Richard, *Images from the floating world*, Fribourg, Switzerland and London, 1978.

Liberty's fans, ancient and modern, Eastern and Western, London, 1894.

Liberty's 1875-1975, Victoria and Albert Museum, London, 1975.

Maignan, Michel, 'Oji & uchiwa', *Bulletin association Franco-Japonaise*, Paris, No. 18, October 1987, pp. 4-17.

Van der Meyden, Hans, 'Some Japanese fan paintings in the Rijksmuseum', *Mededelingenblad van het Rijksmuseum voor Volkenkunde*, Amsterdam, February 1984, pp. 12-16.

Ministère de la culture et de la communication, *Le Japonisme*, Paris, 1988.

Mizuo, Hiroshi, *Edo painting: Sōtatsu and Kōrin*, New York and Tokyo, 1972.

Nakamura, Kiyoe, and others, *Nihon no mon'yo: ōgi* ('Japanese motifs: fans'), Kyoto, 1971.

Nakamura, Kiyoe, *Nihon no ōgi* ('Japanese fans'), Kyoto, 1946.

Nakamura, Kiyoe, *Ōgi to ōgie* ('Fans and fan painting'), Kyoto, 1969.

Newland, Amy and Uhlenbeck, Chris (eds.), *Ukiyo-e to shin hanga*, Wigston, Leicester and London, 1990.

Okudaira, Hideo, *Emaki: Japanese picture scrolls*, Rutland, Vermont and Tokyo, 1962.

von Ragué, Beatrix, *A History of Japanese lacquerwork*, Toronto and Buffalo, 1976.

Rein, J. J., *The Art industries of Japan*, London, 1894.

Salwey, Charlotte M., *Fans of Japan*, London, 1894.

Salwey, Charlotte M., 'On Japanese fans', *Transactions and proceedings of the Japan society*, Vol. II, London, 1894, pp. 1-3.

Sato, Tomoko and Watanabe, Toshio (eds.), *Japan and Britain, an aesthetic dialogue, 1850-1930*, London, 1991.

Schaap, Robert (ed.), *Meiji, Japanese art in transition*, Leiden, 1987.

Scheurleer, Pauline Lunsingh, 'Fans in 19th century Japan' *Mededelingenblad van het Rijksmuseum voor Volkenkunde*, Amsterdam, February 1984, pp. 7-11.

Stanley-Baker, Joan, *Japanese art*, London, 1984.

Strange, Edward F., *The Colour-prints of Hiroshige*, London, 1925, chapter IX, 'The fan Colour-prints'.

Takeda, Tsuneo, *Nanzenji senmen byōbu* ('Fan leaf screens at the Nanzenji'), Kyoto, 1973.

Thoren, Barbara, 'The Japanese fan', *Arts of Asia*, July-August 1979, pp. 81-87.

Umehara, Professor Munetaka, 'Multifacets of the Japanese fan', *Hilton Horizon*, Vol. 7, No. 2, Winter issue 1985, pp. 10-21.

Wichmann, Siegfried, *Japonisme*, London, 1981.

Wooliscroft Rhead, G., *The History of the fan*, London, 1910, section on Japan, pp. 60-76.

Yoshida, Mitsukuni, *Kyō no uchiwa* ('Round fans of Kyoto'), Kyoto, 1978.

Glossary

Bian Mian ('screen fan') Chinese term for a rigid, fixed fan which could conveniently be held in the hand.

Bombori ('hand lantern') A type of folding fan with guards that curve sharply inwards at the end opposite the rivet. This serves to hold the folded fan leaf, or leaves, firmly together.

Brisé ('broken') French term for a type of folding fan made up of flat sticks, usually of wood or ivory in Japan, which are held together at one end by a rivet and at the other by a thread or ribbon.

Cabriolet A type of folding fan with one or more concentric paper or silk leaves.

Cha No Yu ('hot water for tea') The term usually employed in Japanese for the Tea Ceremony.

Cockade Fan A type of *brisé* fan which opens out to form a circle, with the rivet at the centre of the circle. The guards are longer than the other sticks and form the handles of the fan when fully open.

Gofun White pigment made from powdered lead or shell.

Guards The end sticks of a folding fan which are usually thicker than the other sticks and are frequently decorated.

Gumpai Uchiwa ('military fan') A rigid fan made of iron, hardened leather or lacquered wood, frequently decorated with the sun, moon and constellations of the stars.

Gunsen ('war fan') A type of folding fan made up of iron or lacquer sticks and thick paper leaves. It is usually decorated on one side with a painted red sun on a gold ground, and a silver moon on a black ground on the other. Also known as *tessen*.

Hamaguri Uchiwa ('clam fan') A rigid fan made of wood or embroidered silk stretched over a wooden frame. It was so called after its resemblance to the shape of a clam.

Hinoki Cypress wood.

Hiōgi ('cypress fan') A specific type of *brisé* fan which was made of cypress wood and decorated with designs prescribed for use in court circles.

Hiramakie ('flat sprinkled picture') A lacquer technique whereby gold, silver or coloured powder is sprinkled on to a lacquer ground, before it has hardened, to form elements of the design. These leave slightly raised areas and the whole surface is then covered with transparent lacquer.

Hosen ('treasured fan') A small heart-shaped rigid fan associated with the Tōshōdaiji Temple, Nara, where they are scattered by worshippers every year on 19th May.

Imari A type of porcelain for the Western market, characterized by decoration in underglaze blue, overglaze red enamel and gilding. The name derives from the port through which ceramics of this type were exported, though they were, in fact, made in at least 11 different kilns.

Inrō ('seal basket') A small container made up of a number of interlocking sections and worn suspended from the sash of the *kimono*. It was frequently made of lacquered wood, and became the focus of great decorative attention.

Japonisme The fashion for Japan and Japanese art in Europe and America at the end of the 19th century. This manifested itself in both an intense interest in Japanese art and the influence of this on indigenous arts, crafts and design.

Kabuki The popular theatre of Japan which originated in the 17th century.

Kimono ('worn thing') Generic term for the traditional Japanese garment of dress.

Kirigane ('cut gold') Flat pieces of gold or other metal, usually cut into small squares and inlaid individually into a wet lacquer ground, frequently producing a mosaic effect.

Maiōgi ('dance fan') A type of folding fan, frequently with lead weights inserted in the guards, used by all types of dancers, including actors in the Kabuki and Noh theatre.

Maki Uchiwa ('roll fan') A type of rigid fan which could, in fact, be rolled around the central stick.

Mita Ōgi ('giant fan') A large type of cockade fan used in processions.

Mizu Uchiwa ('water fan') A type of rigid fan which was specially treated to make it impermeable to water. The fan was used by dipping it in water and, when agitated, it helped to keep the bearer cool by the process of evaporation.

Mokkan A ceremonial accessory, used by court officials during the Nara period, which consisted of wooden slips covered with writing.

Mon Family crest of an artistocratic or samurai family.

Nekome ('cat's eyes') A type of pierced decoration, found on the guards of a fan, which resembles the eyes of a cat.

Noh The classical drama of Japan.

Obi Sash worn with a *kimono*.

Ōgi Generic term for a fan. It may also refer specifically to a folding fan as opposed to an *uchiwa* or rigid fan.

Ojime ('sliding bead') A bead with a central hole through which cords were threaded.

Satsuma A type of pottery characterized by its cream-coloured body, later pieces were elaborately decorated in multi-coloured enamels. The name derives from the province of Satsuma where much of this pottery originated.

Seven Gods of Good Luck (*Shichi fukujin*) A pantheon of seven divinities charged with specific functions for the well-being of humanity.

Shibayama A family of craftsmen, founded in the 18th century, who specialized in *inrō* decoration. Their work is characterized by minute pieces of inlay, often carved, and applied to a base material so that they stand in relief.

Shibu Uchiwa ('persimmon juice fan') A rigid fan used in the kitchen to revive the embers of a stove.

Shubi A fan-like object preserved in the Shōsōin imperial repository, at the Tōdaiji Temple, Nara.

Suehiro ('wide-ended') A type of folding fan which resembles a Y-shape when closed. This was caused by the guards being splayed out, slightly pulling out the folds of the paper or silk leaves.

Sugi Cedar wood.

Sutra (Sk: *sūtra*, J: *kyo* or *gyo*) A sacred Buddhist text.

Takamakie ('high sprinkled picture') As *hiramakie* but here areas of the design are raised in relief by means of adding a material such as charcoal powder, or a compound of grinding-powder, and raw lacquer before the sprinkled metal powders.

Tantō Fan This was not a fan, but a *tantō* dagger in a sheath which resembled a closed folding fan.

Tendai A sect of Esoteric Buddhism which was introduced to Japan by Saicho (767-822).

Tessen ('iron fan') See under *gunsen*.

Tōsenkyo A fan game which involves attempts to knock a weighted target off a stand by throwing a folding fan at it.

Tsuba Sword guard.

Tuan Shan ('round fan') Chinese term for a rigid, fixed fan which was mounted on a long pole and used as a ceremonial fan at important functions and processions.

Uchiwa ('round fan') The generic term for a rigid, fixed fan.

Ukiyoe ('floating world pictures') Paintings and woodblock prints of the 17th to 19th centuries which depict the 'floating world' of urban pleasures.

Index

Please note: each full Japanese name is listed under the name by which the individual is most commonly known in the West and not necessarily by their surname.